Improve Vocabulary

Pronounce Sight Words to Improve Vocabulary Skills

(Improve Your Reading Skills the Fun Way and Boost Your Vocabulary)

Joseph Reynolds

Published By **Ryan Princeton**

Joseph Reynolds

Improve Vocabulary: Pronounce Sight Words to Improve Vocabulary Skills (Improve Your Reading Skills the Fun Way and Boost Your Vocabulary)

ISBN   978-1-998927-69-2

No part of this guidebook shall be reproduced in any form without permission in writing from the publisher except in the case of brief quotations embodied in critical articles or reviews.

Legal & Disclaimer

The information contained in this book is not designed to replace or take the place of any form of medicine or professional medical advice. The information in this book has been provided for educational & entertainment purposes only.

The information contained in this book has been compiled from sources deemed reliable, and it is accurate to the best of the Author's knowledge; however, the Author cannot guarantee its accuracy and validity and cannot be held liable for any errors or omissions. Changes are periodically made to this book. You must consult your doctor or get professional medical advice before using any of the suggested remedies, techniques, or information in this book.

Table Of Contents

Chapter 1: Why Improve Your English Fluency

Being understood without a doubt.

Basically, at the same time as you communicate nicely, humans could be able to recognize you higher and in reality. When you talk very rapid, then human beings will no longer understand a single phrase that you say. Also, if you communicate properly, humans may also want to have a higher records of the message that you need to impose. For instance, if you mumble, humans have to have the have an effect on that you may not need to be there. It may additionally appear to them that you do now not need to talk to them so you are genuinely mumbling in location of making them pay interest what you are actually announcing. But at the same time as you talk in fact, human beings will pay attention to you and they'll honestly recognize the subjects which you are speaking about.

Being a pleasure to pay attention to.

Isn't it right to recognize that human beings enjoy paying attention to the topics that you are speaking approximately? Keep in thoughts that powerful communique additionally is based upon on whether or not or not the intention market is paying attention to you or not. People will no longer listen to you within the occasion that they do now not revel in the revel in of paying attention to you. If you sound frightened, then people will maximum in all likelihood think that you are not organized in handing over your speech. People will expect that you aren't a amazing speaker, because of this undergo in mind you stupid. As a quit end result, they may get bored in what you're pronouncing, and you'll now not be capable of communicate well with them.

Being greater confident.

If you realise in your self that you are a fantastic speaker, then you may most probably increase that self notion each time you've got have been given to talk inside the front of numerous humans. If you extend correct speaking skills, then you will growth self guarantee as nicely. Speaking well ensures that you will not fail due to the truth you're prepared to accomplish that and you recognize what you're doing. This in turn will make you greater assured to speak up and have interaction greater humans to take note of you.

It can be clean to speak whilst you adventure and meet new people.

One of the most interesting benefits of enhancing your English fluency is that you can tour round the arena freely without traumatic approximately conversation troubles. You have the chance to satisfy new human beings every at the same time as mastering in a difficult and rapid and whilst travelling. People usually get greater open and top notch while you speak their language.

Besides, whilst you test a foreign places language or perhaps more than one foreign languages, your alternatives for journeying destinations become extra. It is less complicated to visit a country and to enjoy your live there if you recognize the language. The neighborhood human beings will appreciate that you could speak their mother tongue and it'll open up new opportunities as a manner to test greater about different humans's lives and cultures.

And as you understand, the arena is whole of interesting and splendid cultures which can be so unique from each special and every so often so close to each awesome on the same time. Knowing foreign places languages helps you to find out extra and notice the area from a distinct perspective, from a easy mind-set. Believe me, no longer absolutely everyone has the chance to peer all of this, to experience and understand the lives of others, or understand about their history, philosophy, and their manner of living and loving. People who've the hazard to adventure the world have a greater appreciation for the finer subjects life has to provide.

Your brain strength is boosted.

Because a language is an entire new complicated device that consists of grammar, vocabulary, similarly to large guidelines and structures, your brain has to retrain itself to think. It has to absorb and assimilate it all. As a end result, your mind starts going for walks greater intensively, and your cognitive thinking, vital questioning, and hassle-solving competencies begin to evolve.

When speakme English, one constantly has to select appropriate wording and phrases to specific themselves in a significant way. Different languages have one-of-a-kind nuances, idiomatic expressions, and meanings. Hence the speaker has to choose phrases and systems from the variety that they will understand and negotiate the which means earlier than the use of a word in a sentence or a word. This includes large trouble-solving approaches and needs exercising and similarly exercise.

Your reminiscence is more.

The greater you operate your brain, the higher it will serve you. Improving your fluency doesn't definitely comprise being able to use special systems, policies, phrases, and sentences, it additionally entails remembering the manner to apply all the aforementioned topics. That is why people who keep close a couple of languages usually recollect names, guidelines, and locations better than people who keep near simplest their nearby language.

One extra detail to note regarding multilingual human beings is that distinctive studies display that those who recognize more than one language have very sharp minds, i.E. They must study matters higher than monolinguals.

Your mom language improves.

We not often assume earlier than we utter a word or a phrase in our mom tongue. We use the grammatical structures and the vocabulary that we've constructed up over years, and we collect this robotically. However, even as studying a foreign places language, we begin evaluating it with the only we already apprehend. As a end result, we start paying extra interest to the grammar, vocabulary, punctuation, and shape of our nearby language. This revel in provides us with the possibility to beautify our mother tongue as properly. As a give up result, we become better communicators, listeners, and editors. These abilties definitely help us in our ordinary existence.

You turn out to be actual at one-of-a-kind subjects too.

Learning a new language lets in enhance your average overall performance in wonderful topics too. Different research endorse that multilingual human beings get immoderate ratings on severa standardized exams, in addition to listening and comprehension sports, in comparison to monolingual people.

You get higher career opportunities.

Employers like employees who can communicate nicely. For you this indicates you could have a more quantity of career opportunities. The majority of employers assume that fluent personnel add cost to the workplace and that their abilties are crucial for an business enterprise or a organisation.

Being capable of deliver authority.

When you talk with a steadier voice because of this that authority, humans will in turn take you critically, questioning which you have an expert over them. Moreover, whilst you're the chief to your university or to your paintings, your humans will then get hold of as real with that you have authority over them because of the fact you talk authoritatively.

Being capable of entertain people.

Speaking properly can sooner or later entertain your target marketplace and maintain their hobby for your speech. Always keep in mind that brilliant your target market is in reality considered one in all your goals even as speaking. It makes you consider your listeners and the way you will be capable of preserve them interested by what you are saying as an alternative on just focusing on how actual or terrible your standard overall performance may be. Basically, acceptable speakme talents help in giving your speech a range in terms of the scenario rely extensive variety, quantity, tempo, tone, and others. It furthermore offers you spontaneity, humor, entertainment further to reminiscences or anecdotes as you deliver your speech.

Being capable of build a rapport.

In verbal exchange, it is very critical which you maintain related collectively along side your target audience. Always keep in thoughts that it's miles essential that you recognize your target market and you construct a rapport with them. Good talking skills will in turn interact your target audience to concentrate to you. You is probably able to build accurate relationships with them through effective verbal exchange.

Chapter 2: Understanding Grammar And Pronunciation To Improve Your English Fluency

English has many twists and turns nearly approximately the actual utilization of it. Not even neighborhood English audio system are genuinely privy to all of the technical factors of their tongue, and they will be now not responsible. Not all are crucial for ordinary conversations. Most are best performed in fields like business agency or teachers for the reason that they require a higher diploma and particular manner of talking. The key to an smooth answer is the manner you've got a take a look at the troubles.

Focus at the versions among your nearby language and English

It is simpler to apprehend the whys approximately the way that English is used when you have a have a look at it to your mom language.

There are a few easy sentence introduction rules and expressions which are really there if you want to do as you please with them. But most of those you definitely took on from your dad and mom as a baby without in truth being aware of them. In university although, that modified. You have grow to be privy to the sure patterns that have been continuously there, and that you in no manner questioned as it all got here manifestly to you.

Now you need to use this, in terms of English. Ask your self, what are the variations among my language and English? Is it in the production of the sentences? A accurate instance for that is the adjective's role. In a few languages, the substantives come in advance than the adjectives even as in English is clearly the alternative.

Another hassle is the verb tenses. The first-rate way to address this is with the resource of locating for each verbal time and tenses its representative in your language. Because some of them can be clearly wonky, like the precise progressive form for the destiny stressful. Some languages in truth don't have a specific grammatical version for that. Something else to hold in thoughts right right here is to have a study the beyond tenses for the most ordinary verbs, as they arrive in available, and the overall production of instances. Like, using will alongside a verb to explicit the future; whilst to apply do, have or has. There are crucial topics whilst expressing yourself in English.

Some type of a novelty is the phrasal verbs which you've without a doubt met already. It's essentially a verb, that once paired with an adverb or preposition, their because of this modifications absolutely. Let's see an instance of this.

• Take-is a verb that expresses the motion of attaining and protecting a few issue, or disposing of some element from a selected place.

• Take aside-approach to split a few element into top notch portions.

• Take off-can talk to removing a chunk of clothing or no longer going to work for a term.

• Take over-it method to take manage of something.

• Take up - ought to signify something that fills your location or time or the begin of a contemporary normal activity like cooking.

And so on. Unfortunately, the ones are also some detail that you'll need to investigate. If you've got been diligent along with your previous duties, you likely already discovered what phrasal verbs are used on a crucial degree. Next time you watch a film or study a ebook, attempt to be aware down each phrasal verb, together collectively together with your rationalization of its which means that. Keep them round and test them every now and then to make certain that the statistics stays inside the energetic reminiscence, and not stored spherical as forgettable.

Look up idioms

Idioms are proverbs and expressions that inside the essential all languages have. It's normally the vintage folks who use them the most, but there are various that have confident their area as an vital part of the not unusual language.

You have them too in your native language and you'll be surprised at how everyday they will be. They won't have the same genuine shape or phrases, however the because of this is form of the equal. It's a one-of-a-type and interesting component to study, how languages vary but have such masses of things in commonplace.

Try to keep song of all the idioms that you manage to go back round at the equal time as searching movies, reading a ebook, and so on. Jot them down on a piece of paper or for your telephone and appearance them up later.

Make it a hint enterprise in case you want. Think first of what you located that idiom technique and supply your self elements on a scale from 1 to 10 for a manner close have been you to the real which means. Set a number of your preference as a each day motive and strive your quality to attain it. It's a nice little activity to revel in alongside pals and circle of relatives that's sure to motive some laughs.

Watch YouTube tutorials to decorate your pronunciation

Somebody as quickly as said that you can discover some issue on YouTube, and that all people have emerge as right. This video platform is a heaven for people who are searching out information. That's a tremendous element for those who want to enhance their pronunciation.

Just search for your selected English accessory and you need to discover hundreds of beneficial movement photographs. It's extraordinary if you encompass terms like "beginner" and "for starters." If you are not sure which accessory fits you great, YouTube can once more offer you with a supporting hand. Try typing a few component like "American VS British English," and that should give you a pleasing level of assessment.

A not unusual belief is that American English is a good deal much less hard to speak and understand while the British is taken into consideration the "fancy" manner to go. Try no longer to be due to method of manner of popular evaluations. Make your hobby a tad less complicated and pick for your self after a small creation to the primary differences.

Grammar isn't always any smooth organization I apprehend, however I'm afraid it can't be avoided. Like it or no longer, you can't in fact have a look at a language without doing a sweep of the technical additives of it. Or, anyways, you will communicate a botched up English that won't do you any favors. So, be affected individual even as coping with those troubles. If you examine the previous hints, you could get via this with out a issues.

Also, don't get stuck on this step. You can usually come once more to it later when you have extra time available. Anyway, a number of the notions will should be found and forgotten a few instances earlier than you could proudly say which you have mastered them.

Great device for purchasing this an extended manner already. I'm fine you've advanced lots due to the fact you've picked up this e-book. Now comes the ultimate check for you, wherein you may see precisely in which you stand right now together along with your getting to know manner.

Chapter 3: The Influence Of The Mother Tongue On English As A Second Language

The mother tongue or the native language is the language that a person speaks as a dominant language. When someone begins learning a ultra-modern language, the mom tongue can also have an effect on the latest language in numerous strategies. As a cease end result, the language learner may additionally furthermore experience reserved and burdened due to which have an impact on thinking about that it could display up in their forms of writing and speech. Let us now bear in mind numerous examples in which the close by language affects the remote places language.

In maximum times, the mother tongue affects the manner you, as a learner of a trendy language, use grammar and the way you shape a sentence. For example, many humans try to translate expressions and idioms from their local language to English. As , at the same time as humans translate constant expressions, those expressions hardly ever make sense. Each language has its own precise language shape and speech patterns. Try translating "hit the nail on the pinnacle" truly into Spanish, for example, and then ask a nearby Spanish speaker if the interpretation method some factor to them at all. How approximately "via manner of the pores and pores and skin of my teeth" or "chew the bullet?" How might also the ones turn out in French? How about Russian?

It is now and again truly hard to end up privy to the neighborhood language have an impact on for the cause that speaker might not have determined out the best grammar rules or expressions. It must moreover be noted that precise local languages get stimulated with the aid of the usage of English in special processes. That's why we can't certainly make a list of all of the commonplace mistakes that non-local audio system make while speaking in English. The following are the topics that is probably recommended with the resource of the local language:

- The sentence shape and word order

- Syntax

- Grammar guidelines (verb paperwork, adjectives and adverbs, tenses, and mood)

- The selection of vocabulary devices, terms, expressions, and idioms

- Punctuation

- Pronunciation of numerous phrases and sounds

The aspect with pronunciation is in fact essential. There are languages that lack a number of the sounds that make up the English alphabet, and vice versa. For example, Germans occasionally confuse "w" with "v" and pronounce a word like "properly" as "vell." The French and the Russians are not used to pronouncing the "h" sound nicely. Russians commonly pronounce the aggregate "th" in English phrases both as "d" or as "z." Vowels might also pose a problem for a native Chinese speaker because of the massive distinction amongst Chinese vowel sounds and English vowel sounds.

Some greater examples of local language have an effect on consist of the following:

• The language learner won't distinguish sure English sounds due to their neighborhood language and, therefore, might not be capable of pronounce them in English.

• The language learner may probably substitute numerous native language sounds with those who appear comparable (however now not same) in English. For instance, the Russian sound "r" may be used in location of the English "r" and so forth. The Chinese typically substitute their "ei" with the English "e."

- Usually, the language green people upload useless vowels either in the middle or at the give up of a phrase this is hard for them to pronounce because of the numerous consonants in it.

- The language learner may moreover supply their close by language strain to the ultra-present day language. As a prevent stop result, their terms may sound bizarre with surprising emphasis and hard to understand.

- Another state of affairs associated with the problem of strain is that the language green men and women is probably not able to not stress the unstressed vowels. If this takes place, double-stress may be heard in a unmarried short word.

- The language learner can also convey along with her or him the standard tone of voice, sentence tempo, and intonation of his/her local language to the foreign places language. The identical applies to the voice and the manner his or her mouth works whilst announcing unique sounds. For example, numerous languages comprise a touch nasality even as others do no longer have that feature.

To sum up, the complete concept of mother tongue have an impact on is that the sounds of your nearby language seep into your new language, and this may be for quite some reasons. For example, you can't have listened to enough English speech, or you may no longer have spoken an entire lot in English, or no person has ever tried to accurate your pronunciation or different language errors in modern day. Mother tongue have an impact on can, of course, be regular via tough artwork and exercising. Hence, if you as a speaker experience that you do no longer sound accurate and you understand which you want to perform a little issue along with your language to make it sound extra English-like, you need to comply with our recommendations on getting rid of the local tongue have an impact on and finally beating the accessory.

What is an accent and do I without a doubt have one?

Sometimes it's far absolutely difficult to be aware whether or not you do have an accent or not. At least, for you it's far. The majority of those who look at English assume that they do no longer have an accent however they arrive from a whole lot of cultures and communicate superb languages that in fact have some have an effect on on the stylish language they're analyzing. But the query is why don't people note they even though have an accessory? The reason for this is because of the fact they come to be so centered at the content material material cloth of what they're going to mention that they end up distracted from its shape and the way it all sounds. Let's have a have a take a look at numerous records regarding your accent:

The accessory is anywhere

Anyone speaks with an accessory, whether they recognise it even as on foot round their homeland or no longer. As quick as you eliminate your accessory, people will now not ask you to replicate phrases and phrases so you can understand what you are saying. However, this doesn't recommend that this fashionable American English isn't an accessory. It is the accessory of North America which might be difficult to understand in the south or in other worldwide locations in which English is being spoken as a mother tongue with a unique accessory.

And you could no longer pay hobby yours

As I said above, it is normal to now not be aware your very very own accessory. But what isn't ordinary is not even searching out to enhance your accent irrespective of how well you talk English. It could be very similar to cooking. You can also assume that you are cooking pretty properly till your companion says that the dishes you prepare dinner are every now and then absolutely salty. It's the same at the side of your accent. You won't phrase it until someone tells you about it.

One reason why we may not examine our non-public accent is that as we grow older, our brains start narrowing down their belief of diverse sounds. For instance, a touch little one may also moreover revel in the distinction many of the unique pronunciations of "r" than a grown-up person. So, right right here is the truth we ought to deal with.

It relies upon on who you socialize with most

Usually, the those who most experience that they need to improve their pronunciation and to do away with the accessory from their speech are folks who socialize masses with native English audio device. Through evaluation, they see that their English differs from others in masses of strategies, and, as a result, the need arises to improve the language. Additionally, the ones individuals who do understand that they have an accent try to resemble the native audio tool. That's why their accent is milder in comparison to precise human beings's accents who don't come to this interest.

Chapter 4: How To Improve Your Speaking Skills

Have you ever felt so concerned whenever you have got to talk inside the front of humans? Have you ever had your knees and fingers shake every time you are status within the the front of your goal marketplace? Do now not worry. It isn't always the forestall of the sector for you!

There will usually come a time in your existence wherein you need to enlarge your boundaries. There is probably a time in which you have to pass from speaking to surely one particular character, allow us to mention your buddy or your determine, to addressing a massive group of human beings, allow us to mention your entire magnificence on your lecture elegance or the humans on your paintings employer. The concept is that talking to the overall public intention market is inevitable.

But in the first region, why are we afraid of speakme in public?

It can be due to the reality we assume that humans couldn't care less approximately what we're going to talk about. We experience like as soon as we start speakme, they may actually be yawning and be equipped that lets in you to give up your speech with the intention to have their freedom. Or probable you had a traumatic revel in within the beyond in which you've have been given been humiliated while talking inside the the front of human beings.

However, the ones must now not restriction you from talking up. Now is the proper time in order to understand how you may be able to enhance your competencies in talking and knock all of your fears away.

In this monetary destroy, we are in a position to talk about the strategies you will be able to beautify your speaking skills a terrific way to improve your English fluency. We might also even very well talk how you'll be able to knock out your fear of speakme in public after which talk up so that you can have better possibilities on your profession and to your lifestyles.

If there's one all-important factor to make approximately talking, it's that so that you can gather conversational fluency, you need to exercising talking loads. It doesn't remember if you begin speakme from day one or after a 3 hundred and sixty five days of enter, that is an inevitable fact that might't be averted. Communicating with others is the primary motive most human beings observe a language, however it's additionally the unmarried capacity that human beings conflict the most with starting, in factor because of the truth it can appear absolutely frightening if you've by no means executed it earlier than. This worry is sincerely natural, however it's nearly completely unfounded and you could't permit it save you you.

One large fear which gives to the concern that a few people have in terms of speakme (specifically if beginning early) is the concept of "fossilization." Fossilization is the concept that on the identical time as you repeat a mistake typically, it turns into ingrained in your speech and also you'll by no means be able to repair it. However, even though it's possible that some fossilization would possibly upward thrust up, this worry is largely unfounded for 2 big reasons:

• No depend how extended you take a look at in advance than you begin talking, while you do start to talk, you will make mistakes, a number of that you received't be privy to until/in the occasion that they're pointed out. Your mind is so busy seeking to produce the language that it could with out hassle bypass over a mistake while you make it even if you already recognize the ideal way to mention it. This takes area all of the time with even my top-intermediate and in any other case superior students who clearly haven't quite had sufficient talking exercising however who have commonly incredible English capability.

- The extraordinary big reason why you shouldn't worry is that being corrected isn't typically the amazing difficulty. Every proper language trainer is privy to that after the pupil has a low speakme degree, many errors need to simply be not noted so long as they don't avoid verbal exchange. This is because of the truth if the trainer attempted to accurate each little mistake, it'd most probable sooner or later demotivate the scholar although they determine upon that the entirety be corrected.

In truth, it may forestall the development of the pupil thru making them hyper-vigilant no longer to make any errors that's disastrous. As the pupil improves, greater errors ought to be corrected, but the attention of correction is on larger devices until the pupil reaches better tiers at which detail every little mistake need to be corrected. In particular phrases, regardless of whether or not fossilization is a trouble or no longer, making mistakes is inevitable so it's commonly not something to worry about.

Anyone who tells you which you shouldn't begin talking for fear of fossilization doesn't recognize what they're speakme about.

So, whilst you first begin speaking, you need to consciousness more on fluidity and speakme as loads as you can (massive talking) in the route of your conversations, however take the comments which you get and use it to decorate the accuracy (huge talking) outside of conversations or from time to time inner conversations/one-on-one lessons via supplemental accuracy exercise, that could take many paperwork, as we'll see later.

As you get greater snug speakme, you'll have accumulated a high-quality essential quantity of exercising and you may slowly start moving the focal point from fluidity to accuracy so that you can take away any lingering mistakes.

Whatever you do and irrespective of even as you choose to begin talking, ensure to speak as tons and regularly as you may and maintain going until matters start to "click on on," paying more attention on the start to the larger errors that have an effect on communication rather than the smaller facts of perfection.

Speaking Techniques and Activities

Prepare in advance

Preparing in advance, especially at the same time as you're virtually beginning to speak (and maximum specifically in case you're beginning speaking early) may be extraordinarily useful. The notable element right right right here is that there are a ton of factors that you could do and you could pick out one or more of those devices at any time, making them very bendy for plenty wonderful human beings.

Self-advent

The first problem you could do is to create a self-introduction. It's a tremendous component to do each time you begin speakme – whether or now not or no longer that be from day one or day 100 and 80. The cause for this is which you'll be the use of it again and again yet again as you talk to big people. If making a decision to attention on having sincerely one exchange partner or train, then glaringly you acquired't be the use of it over and over, but in all different times, it's a brilliant concept, especially if you decide to tour to a rustic wherein the language is spoken. By memorizing or partly memorizing this in advance than you even begin speaking, you'll have something first of all, as a way to additionally assist to beautify your self belief a piece at the same time as on the identical time allowing the opposite character to examine a chunk about you which can come to be the basis for further verbal exchange.

Topic-based fluency

If you decide to awareness on problem count number-primarily based totally honestly fluency, you may exercising speaking approximately some thing subject matter(s) you're focusing on. The high-quality component about that is which you don't sincerely should have masses of experience or modern statistics to start speakme. Learn some crucial grammar and a few unique vocabulary related to a selected subject matter. You can start talking right away as you're learning these items, or you could prepare and building up a few facts a chunk first after which start speaking about it.

Remember that you may flow into as deep into the project as you want or need (a notable way to take you thru increasingly more specific vocabulary), but the better you flow into, you may run right into a need for some greater complicated grammar. This obtained't be a huge trouble, as you can in reality examine the systems you want in context in desire to doing a gaggle of expert "studying," but it's some thing to hold in thoughts.

In fact, you may create an entire self-examine direction for yourself in this foundation on my own and lay out a street map to have a observe (getting the help of a instructor to plot out what you'll need to research in phrases of grammar might be useful in case you're now not positive).

Talk about making ready beforehand! Now you'll recognize precisely what to analyze and even as which permits you to normally be organized for conversations (even though within the starting you received't quite be having full conversations, however as a substitute practicing the basics of what you're mastering).

Prompts

The next element you could do is to apply activates. These are more commonly used for writing, however you could additionally use them for speaking.

If making a decision on particular questions or maybe a subject matter before your subsequent verbal exchange, you can look up any terms you will in all likelihood want, possibly even a piece of grammar, and prepare an concept of what you need to speak about. You may even do that first on your community language to decide out what you'd like to mention inside the target language. If you need, you can write out your response in the cause language as a few special manner to prepare.

Targeting weaknesses

Whether it's weaknesses that you're aware about or weaknesses which may be mentioned to you, they may need to be addressed in more than one area, together with speaking. For example, if you have some grammar troubles, it is probably which you're certainly bizarre with a specific grammar idea due to the reality you haven't discovered it however, or it is probably that you comprehend the form, probably even perfectly, but you haven't activated it however.

In the primary case, you have were given ranges to paintings on: the initial studying (passive knowledge) and being able to use what you've discovered (active utility).

Of course, you can do both of those on the same time, and that's what a few human beings pick out out over too much formal have a study. In stylish, notwithstanding the fact that, a chunk of coaching and take a look at time whilst you've emerge as privy to the issue can pass an extended way and will without a doubt help prepare your mind to investigate the material better every in the course of and after the following verbal exchange.

So, one outstanding use of it slow outside of conversations (and possibly the exceptional use of it sluggish if you're going an output direction or have reached an output phase) is to hobby on strengthening your vulnerable elements in passive knowledge, some thing they will be, and then try and set off them in the following verbal exchange. And don't overlook about to use the eighty/20 rule which we'll come once more to at the cease of the bankruptcy.

Weaknesses that you may reason consist of: sure vocabulary, unique grammar structures, the usage of connectors, and so on... You can also paintings on very precise factors of pronunciation, however recollect that searching out to have exquisite pronunciation inside the route of a communication is a recipe for disaster. I'd possibly maintain one or mainly hard sounds in mind at the same time as talking, collectively with the "r" sound, however don't allow it derail your conversation.

Talk across the terms you don't recognize or can't consider

Formally called "circumlocution," this technique is in fact crucial. It's the important problem to accomplishing any sort of fluency and it requires having a effective stage of consolation with being uncomfortable.

This doesn't propose that you need to pass whole throttle thru the whole conversation. In addition, subjects might be quite hard on the start, even though the more you have got were given were given conversations and hire this method, the faster you'll enhance and it'll come to be less complicated in a fantastically brief length of popular speak time.

The cause why this method is so powerful and essential is that it forces you to forestall counting on your neighborhood language, at least inside the course of the time which you're alleged to be working towards your goal language. It's one manner of forcing your thoughts to comply.

At instances it may be pretty irritating, however live with it and also you'll achieve the rewards. One of the largest reasons why this approach is so high-quality is that it forces you to try and use related terms, further to the grammar essential to supply your message which strengthens your common capability to link phrases or even thoughts collectively inside the language.

Talking to your self and thinking within the language

Many of the following points can exercise in addition to each questioning inside the language and speaking to your self so I've located them into the identical organisation proper right here. Talking to yourself may sound loopy, however it's virtually not. Besides, I'm not telling you to absolutely speak out loud even as on foot down the street (greater on that during a minute). You can try this at the same time as you're by myself – especially within the bathe – and also you don't even need to be specially loud.

Some people, however, are afraid of self-speak for a awesome cause: fossilization. The concept goes that in case you spend too much time speakme to your self, you'll have a disproportionate quantity of output to remarks so you can lead you to growing eternal errors at the manner to be hard or not possible to take away on the equal time as you're greater superior.

Though I do see a few advantage to this, so long as you're continuously mastering and in search of to decorate, it shouldn't be an lousy lot of a trouble, specifically in case you're virtually doing it to try to get some extra exercising among conversations.

One of the terrific benefits of this workout is finding wherein your holes are, this is authentic of conversation in desired, but in this case, you don't want a associate or trainer to find out the ones holes which can be more obvious, together with unknown terms or large grammar elements. You'll additionally always run into questions about all styles of subjects associated with every vocabulary and grammar, in addition to some pronunciation so make sure to write down all of these devices down so that you can both appearance them up or ask about them later.

Another advantage of this is that it let you get more comfortable simply saying terms and sentences and having them go with the go together with the waft out of your mouth. This is honestly a splendid talking exercising technique and might help your pronunciation, as properly, if you're specializing in pronouncing it as perfectly as you could. You can also use it to rehearse or exercising for your subsequent conversation if the challenge is deliberate or you have an idea for what you need to talk about. You can even use this time to beautify the remarks you previously acquired and/or exercise newly determined out grammar standards.

In short, self-communicate can be approximately some thing and everything or focused topics, and ideally you want to try this as lots as you could. If you're on an output-based path, this is particularly beneficial, however for an enter-based totally route, it could be a supplementary hobby that will help you spark off some of what you're analyzing. Have fun and play with language!

In phrases of thinking within the language in desire to talking within the language, this can be quite tough at the begin, even though one trouble I've located is that the greater steady and engaged input you have were given, the extra willing your mind is to surely or even spontaneously do it. With that in thoughts, your quantity of output within the shape of verbal exchange will efficiently restrict exactly what thoughts you may string together, as talking to yourself is definitely the quiet, intellectual model of speaking. You moreover lose the gain of tracking and tweaking your pronunciation it sincerely is a possible opportunity that talking to yourself can offer because of the reality you've got got greater time and much a whole lot much less pressure outdoor of an actual conversation.

Shadowing to assist with pace and simplicity of speech

This method is absolutely at once associated with pronunciation, but one trouble I've discovered from private experience is that shadowing also can help you produce speech greater rapid. There's a stability right right here. After you shadow something enough, you'll end up memorizing it, which genuinely isn't terrible, however that's now not the purpose for talking.

However, if you exercise shadowing to specific problems that you have, including hard intonation patterns or hard sound clusters, then it'll assist now not only your pronunciation plenty, but additionally how speedy and without problems you may communicate.

Keeping breaks in thoughts a excellent way to keep away from burnout, the aggregate of these can sincerely supercharge your efforts and stress your mind to conform even further. Depending on the balance making a decision to put into effect (50/50 input and output, extra input, or more output), this may be greater green and sustainable for specific humans, so, as always, in case you're interested in this kind of technique, find what mixture works top notch for you.

Learning from conversations

This is essentially unique in a single thing, which is which you no longer most effective find out new phrases and phrases, but you get corrections and unique varieties of remarks which in turn assist you show wherein your weaknesses lie so you can intention them. And no longer just grammar corrections, however phrase corrections and phrase/sentence corrections, making them extraordinarily valuable.

In addition to virtually getting corrections on the right words and terms, you furthermore may also moreover get comments on what sounds herbal. Even between languages which might be exceedingly similar, along with Spanish and English, or even Spanish and Portuguese (which might be highly comparable), what sounds natural won't constantly be as smooth as converting the phrases from one language to another even though the grammar could be very comparable.

So, further to any new terms and phrases that you pick out out up thru the verbal exchange, you furthermore mght get feedback in your use of terms (and grammar). One of the brilliant subjects about having a whole lot of conversations over a quick time body is which you'll extra effortlessly maintain in mind subjects.

You need to though hold song, mainly for the ones matters that surely don't seem to paste no matter how usually you come across them in a communique, however due to the fact you're using the language with such a immoderate frequency, that acts to help keep new records sparkling prolonged sufficient for it to get into your long time memory.

80/20 programs

We've already pointed out a number of areas inside the realm of speaking that have eighty/20 programs, specially centered on weaknesses, applying/activating terms and grammar through situation remember-based totally fluency, and self-introductions. Of those, focused on weaknesses is probably the unmarried most treasured factor you could do. Remember to usually ask yourself: "What's the maximum vital problem I absolutely have right now?" It won't be unique to talking or constrained to talking, but it may no matter the truth that be a few component in case you want to impact your speaking a exceptional deal.

Maybe it's a loss of vocabulary in wellknown or on a excessive best difficulty matter, unfamiliarity with a vital grammar concept, or an incapacity to wrap your mouth around difficult corporations of sounds or hit the right intonation whilst crucial.

In essence, eighty/20 packages for speakme will in large part be giant sports activities in preference to first-rate sports activities, especially within the event that they contain any shape of deep exercising. When you zoom out and keep along aspect your conversations, you'll be returned into large mode and can activate a number of what you've discovered thru an entire lot of exercising. In truth, enormous speaking exercise has essential purposes: working toward what you've determined out/are reading and locating more matters to artwork on thru showing you your weaknesses and information gaps.

Just remember now not to get paralyzed with grammar assessment through using the usage of looking for to be perfect. It will come. Just exercise, find and goal weaknesses, and exercise a few more.

To use a language is to change it

Necessity is the mom of invention. When human beings have a hard verbal exchange need, they clearly invent new phrases or use them in a brand new manner. We frequently keep in mind a language as a static set of phrases and meanings. However, language is truly a difficult and fast of personal institutions which get related to a hard and fast of mouth movements and sounds. As we speak, we surely harmonize and agree at the institutions that we use to create our terms. Across our language manner of existence, this takes area at this shape of scale that it is tough to look the huge averaging method this is taking place. Because so masses parents all agree on a fairly similar set of institutions, we neglect about that language is absolutely a non-public manner.

How do you apprehend that what you name the shade blue is the equal colour blue that everyone else sees? You can in no manner understand this due to the reality you could never see thru some different individual's eyes.

When you embody language in a smaller institution length or a more isolated setting, it's far less complicated to look it shifting. This could be very obtrusive in technical groups and in street language. In those environments, the large social agreements for language don't continuously healthy with the communications wishes so the network creates unique jargon or slang. If a set gets isolated for long sufficient, possibly numerous hundred years, they'll even emerge as not able to talk in their precise language.

This is how all of the expected 6,900 languages in the worldwide these days were created.

Language is a hard and fast of shared communique habits that build up over the years. As they boom, they get extra complicated. A word like "no" might likely seem simply clean, but negatives can truly be expressed in complex strategies.

A phrase like "don't prevent considering the purple ball that isn't bouncing" is absolutely an entire bunch of complicated bad mind jammed collectively. To decode this, we want an agreed-upon set of conventions, otherwise the conversation acquired't transmit. Over time, the ones conventions get extra complicated. In a few times, the conventions don't work well, so we agree on an exception.

The trouble is all of the ones times and exceptions. Every language has its private unique method to resolving all instances and exceptions, and there are an awful lot of them. If you try to analyze they all too quick, it will without troubles crush your functionality to speak.

Native audio machine don't commonly recognise the grammar hints; they just talk. They set an cause to speak, open their mouths and terms pop out.

They stay inside the international in their language and were conditioned thinking about a younger age. They NEVER take into account the pointers. This is the essence of what makes this approach effective. The underlying form of any language is mind-numbingly apparent to a neighborhood speaker, but alien to a brand new language learner. In order to assemble spoken language go with the flow, you want to act like a nearby speaker. Spend lots of time Conditioning your Enchants, and the rest will display up robotically.

Knock your worry down

We apprehend that your biggest enemy in phrases of speakme is fear. And while you fear, you hesitate.

Usually, it's far apparent which you are hesitating, or concerned in famous, while you're frequently pronouncing "um" or "er" or one-of-a-kind fillers that are not critical to your speech. Also, your audience can also discover the ones fillers worrying and they'll not be aware of you.

You can also be tripping over your very own phrases occasionally due to the truth are dashing to unique your mind as your mind works faster than your lips. Most of the time, speakme quicker implies which you are fearful.

 For you if you want to knock your hesitations, remember the following steps:

Think extra sincerely.

Doing this could assist you attention on the correct count which you are speaking approximately at the manner to in flip make you talk definitely and properly.

Slow down and emphasize your factors.

It isn't always proper to speak rapid and encounter your phrases as this will handiest make your speech difficult to understand. It is also critical which you emphasize your key points in order that your goal market will recognize wherein your speech is crucial. This may additionally moreover even help you live focused.

Breathe well.

Proper breathing allows you stay relaxed. This may even assist you communicate well just so your target market can be able to recognize you nicely. When it involves dealing with your tension, recall the subsequent guidelines:

Do now not make your nerves ward off you.

Do not continuously cognizance on your self. Think about special audio device getting concerned too! But that isn't the whole factor. Just hold in mind as properly that the humans you're speaking to aren't that aware about how involved you are.

There modified right into a pronouncing as soon as that is going like this: "It is exceptional to have butterflies—as long as they fly in formation."

Connect together with your goal market.

The fulfillment of each communication glide is predicated upon at the results of it to the supposed purpose marketplace. Therefore, because the speaker, it is important which you realize the people who you're going to speak to and you hook up with them. Make superb that you understand their cutting-edge mood as you communicate. If they may be bored, ensure that you are active to type of wake them up.

Have your desires in your mind.

It is important which you recognize why you're talking. Giving speeches isn't simplest approximately disseminating records; it is also about attractive your target audience and giving them what they need.

Always preserve in thoughts your goals or the motive why you're talking. Do you want to entertain people? Do you want to tell or in all likelihood train them?

Be outstanding.

Always reflect onconsideration on succeeding. Imagine your self speakme with a bit of luck and virtually. Paint a photograph of yourself speaking with none flaws or errors. Always attention your mind for your selected very last results, the subjects that you want to attain and now not the matters which you do now not like.

Relax.

Again, it is important that you live cushty at the equal time as you're speakme. Remove all of the tensions, hesitations, and some detail worried for your gadget as you talk. Tell your self with a grin that you are precise enough.

Speak up!

When modified into the very last time you heard a person communicate with authority? With air of mystery? How did you revel in on the equal time as you have got been listening? Did you experience like she or he is a completely credible person, with power and have an effect on?

Speaking nicely might be one of the most commonplace topics that we need to collect. We want to sound authoritative simply so humans will take us as confident and credible audio machine.

This can even make your audience pay more interest to you and to what you are speaking approximately because they locate you influential and powerful.

Stand with self assurance.

Basically, the manner you stand moreover impacts the way you speak. If you stand with a bit of luck, then you may most in all likelihood have the potential to speak with a bit of good fortune as nicely.

People might also even understand you as assured considering that they are able to see you fame with poise; as a cease result, they'll give you their interest. Standing well may even help you produce a better sound or voice whilst talking.

You can beautify your posture as you speak through locating your stability. Have your weight allocated gently between your toes so you will no longer stumble. Stand tall as well and hold your chin lifted up. Doing so additionally presents in your top without any strive.

Moreover, you furthermore mght want to lighten up (how typically have we already emphasized this element on this e book? Oh properly.) and breathe. Release all the anxiety in your face, jaw, neck, and shoulders. Breathe out as properly and allow the air amplify your entire body.

Speak truely.

If you communicate in reality and audibly, you will sound as if you absolutely recommend what you are saying. It will sound like what you are saying comes out of your heart. This may additionally even help you engage your target market to be aware of you due to the fact they understand what you're pronouncing.

Open your mouth nicely as you speak, regardless of the reality which you are not that used to it.

This may additionally furthermore feel uncomfortable in the beginning, however it may moreover come natural to your target market. Practice the mouth exercising as nicely. Make the vowel sounds extra distinguishable and your consonants clearer as properly.

Project nicely.

Therefore, it is important which you challenge your voice in step with the message that you need to impose to your purpose marketplace.

Give emphasis on your key factors.

For you for you to offer your message on your goal market definitely and correctly, it is vital that you emphasize your key factors.

This will allow your target audience understand what are the critical elements of your speech and deliver interest to you as you talk approximately the ones elements. Also, there are times whilst unique speakers supply identical emphasis on each part of their speech due to this making it seem monotonous and boring.

They sound very flat which in flip makes the listeners bored and experience sleepy. If you want to sound authoritative and charismatic, you have to emphasize your terms strongly.

Do no longer rush.

How fast or sluggish you talk could have an impact on the have an impact on you are making among other human beings. If you speak very fast, it could seem like you're excited speakme about that particular hassle depend. People may additionally moreover moreover suppose that you do no longer need to speak to them due to the fact you are dashing matters. On the opposite hand, if you speak slowly, human beings may think of you as uninteresting and they will ultimately get worn-out listening to you.

The component is that you want to display screen the rate of your speech. You neither have to speak rapid or slowly; you want to preserve it sparsely.

Your pace may additionally moreover range, counting on what you're announcing and the message you want to provide on your goal market. Again, you want to emphasize crucial factors so you ought to no longer offer identical weight and tempo to every a part of your speak.

Use your gadgets.

We are talented with unique devices. It virtually is based upon on how we're going to use them to have the capability to speak nicely.

Make your tone difficult or easy, counting on what you need to mention. You also can need to elongate your vowels and use them to specific emotions.

On the alternative hand, use consonants smoothly or sharply to make your speech clearer.

You want to additionally range your pitch; maintain your voice immoderate or deep or everywhere in among, relying on your message.

Use remarkable volumes as properly in that you have to talk loudly in a few a part of your speech and softly in others. There also are a few factors in which you have were given to talk speedy or slowly, depending on the factors you want to emphasise.

Just be high first-rate all of the time.

There isn't always someone else who allow you to but yourself. If you consider your self succeeding, then you'll maximum likely act towards attaining success. Do now not bombard your thoughts with the thoughts that you're going to fail, because of the fact you aren't. You can be successful in case you are decided sufficient that you may be successful!

Chapter 5: Developing Native English Pronunciation To Improve Your English Fluency

Learning a way to pronounce your phrases as a local speaker is one of the toughest factors of getting to know the English language. It does get a good buy easier as you spend more time with English natives. However, to make buddies and get to understand the natives, you have got to be able to speak with them.

On top of all of this, the English language can be pretty complex with phrases, which includes there, their, and they're, manner, whey, and weight, which all sound the equal, but, terms like bomb, comb, and tomb sound virtually remarkable.

The first thing that you want to do is learn how to pay interest nicely. When you're paying attention to podcasts in English, looking movies or looking a television display, ensure that you clearly are listening to what is being said. For example, if someone is speaking, are you in a function to inform if he stated he damage his chin or if he harm his shin? Did the speaker say that he had to get a few sleep or some slips? Being in a function to tell what's being said is going to head an extended way in supporting you discover ways to pronounce the phrases properly and simply so others can understand you.

While you're listening, be aware about how the speaker actions their mouth. Then, while you exercising talking, attain this inside the the the front of a replicate and interest on the way you go with the flow your very personal mouth. You can place one in every of your palms over your mouth as if you were telling a person to "shh" but do no longer get rid of your finger. Instead, experience your lips press towards your finger or shrink back from it.

Pay hobby to the way you waft your tongue as well. You will study that whilst you're speakme English, the simplest distinction inside the phrases rice and brilliant are how you skip your tongue. In order to make the "l" sound, you want to place your tongue on the decrease once more of your pinnacle tooth. Practice announcing the phrase "slight" and be aware about in which your tongue is on your mouth.

When you are pronouncing the letter "r," your tongue should not pass the least bit. The "r" sound is made actually collectively with your lips. Practice saying "right" with out moving the tongue.

In order to say the "th" sound, open your mouth slightly, setting the give up of your tongue on the lowest of your pinnacle teeth. Say "this" and take note of how your tongue moves.

Every word is crafted from syllables. These syllables are sounds that the phrases make together. For example, the word "together" is probably damaged proper proper right down to TO-GETH-ER. When you recognition on breaking the terms down into sounds, you will be able to pronounce them like a community.

Record yourself at the same time as you are talking. Use the digital camera to your laptop. Make exceptional that you don't just use the voice recorder due to the truth it is vital an awesome manner to see the manner that your lips and tongue movements as you speak.

Ask an English speaking buddy, ideally a community, to take a look at the video and correct a few thing that they see wrong with the manner you are announcing your phrases.

Make buddies with a native English speaker and spend time working in the direction of the language in conjunction with her or him as frequently as feasible.

The of you can have amusing training, and you becomes inside the route of your pal. This may additionally additionally even will permit you to revel in assured whilst you communicate due to the truth that the individual you practiced with corrected all your errors.

By surely the usage of the ones pointers, you'll discover that you are announcing your terms better, more like a nearby, humans can be capable of apprehend you more, and you may be capable of talk much less tough with the ones round you.

Practice, memorize, and exercise

It will take art work. Learning to speak fluently is rewiring your ears to listen new sounds, training your mouth to provide new sounds, education your mind to apprehend new grammatical policies and utilising them. This takes repetition.

Too frequently college students aren't able to undergo in thoughts vocabulary phrases, sounds or grammar from a preceding lesson. In this e-book, we are capable of cowl a way to create a effective memorization device to maximise studying, bear in mind an English phrase all the time and efficient techniques to maintain in thoughts pronunciation. Let's get to it.

Producing English sounds

• English pronunciation is broken into three number one disturbing conditions:

• Ear education (Hear and understand sounds)

• Mouth Training (Create sounds)

• Eye education (Spell sounds)

There are 40 sounds in the English language. There are not any terms that don't re-use these sounds.

Learn to recognize, create, and spell those sounds and their combinations. We could have close by English pronunciation. Sounds clean? Wondering how are we able to try this? Read on.

Sounds come from our vocal cords. They push air thru our throat and mouths. Using our tongue, lips, and mouth, we channel this air to create quite a few sounds. In English, sounds are divided into consonants and vowels.

Exploring your very own voice

The human voice is a massive a part of who we're and the manner we perform in society. You carry your voice anywhere your skip; you may't just leave it at home now not like your telephones or your wallets (that you need to no longer depart at domestic as well, however this is already a one-of-a-type story).

And earlier than we even begin mastering a manner to increase a exquisite talking knowledge, it's far important that we find out our very very very own voice first.

Our voice is a completely effective and essential tool that we've got got for it tells precise humans lots of things approximately you. It moreover influences the way humans understand and create impressions about you.

Experts definitely recollect the human voice as a person's "calling card." They say that the voice speaks for your self extra than your clothes or your bodily look do.

Once people pay attention your voice, they mechanically create assumptions about you primarily based on what they've got honestly heard.

Most humans also will be inclined to decide you based totally on the way you speak to them, or essentially on the way you talk.

There are some who suppose that someone isn't authoritative sufficient because of the reality his or her voice seems to be so tender even though the case may be otherwise. There are also some instances in which someone thinks of someone else as rude or disrespectful actually because of the truth what she or he has clearly stated. So seemingly, your voice as well as the way you speak tells different human beings lots about yourself.

Also, those parents which might be assured sufficient to speak in public maximum of the time get more possibilities than those who are not that assured.

Even former United States Secretary of State Colin Powell as quickly as admitted in his autobiography that having the capability to talk in public resultseasily and early in his life made a massive impact on his success. He emerge as even promoted in art work due to the fact he had correct speakme capabilities.

However, it does no longer usually endorse that best the ones oldsters which might be correct in speaking get to succeed in lifestyles. After all, no longer all appropriate audio system are appropriate due to the truth they were born; a few are honed thru practice. In the following chapters, we are in a role to speak the methods on how you may enhance your voice in terms of your speakme abilties.

Chapter 6: The Best Way To Learn English Fluently

To have a take a look at quickly similarly to make certain which you are using English the manner a herbal born citizen could communicate it, you have to surround your self with individuals who talk English.

Speaking English nicely is extra than actually gaining knowledge of from a e-book or application.

While you could spend time that specialize in grammar by myself, doing so will no longer allow you to apprehend how people who speak English as a primary language truely communicate.

Instead, watch tv indicates which may be in English, make pals who talk English, and disclose your self to the language every single day.

You want to additionally ensure that you make it a regular to exercise speaking

English on a each day basis. If you do no longer spend time operating towards every unmarried day, you're in no manner going to in reality apprehend how to talk fluently. You need to create a look at plan, become committed, and apprehend that in case you do now not exercise each day, you may rapid overlook about what you've got got located.

You should moreover tell those spherical you, your friends and circle of relatives approximately your recurring, in addition to your examine plan.

Use them to maintain you responsible, to ensure that you live together with your plan and that you are a success at speakme English fluently.

When you are studying new terms, write them down in a small pocket ebook with their definition. Use those new words in sentences at the same time as you talk every day and do your exceptional to say them at least 3 instances on every occasion you communicate.

Study on the same time as you are the most wakeful. If you're a morning individual, it's miles extraordinary at the manner to have a observe as quick as you awaken inside the morning. On the opportunity hand, if you aren't a morning individual, plan on analyzing inside the afternoon so that you understand your mind is simply unsleeping.

You don't need to create some poetic sentence in the need of speaking eloquently later; in reality focus on the basis in the starting. You can consider it in a good deal the same manner as you'll think about coaching a toddler how to talk any language: you start with the most normally used terms. In the us, the ones are frequently discovered out as sight terms, determined out not via way of sounding out the phrase, however truly via recognizing what the word seems like.

You can try this by way of manner of writing the phrases on index gambling playing playing cards. On the once more of the index card, write the definition of the phrase, further to a sentence the use of the phrase. For one week, then have a chum or family member check you at the terms, definitions, and a way to apply the word in a sentence. During the week, you need to attempt to use the phrases as regularly as feasible. Don't try to analyze too many phrases without delay. Instead, choose out among six and 8 terms to research every week. After a few weeks, you will discover that you are capable of string the phrases together growing actually new sentences.

Make fantastic that you are growing each prolonged-time period and brief-term dreams. Each week, set a purpose of now not pleasant what terms you'll study, however how prolonged you may practice as well. It is likewise critical which you create prolonged-term goals. For example, even as do you advise on being capable of preserve a verbal exchange in English, or at the same time as do you plan on being able to understand slang? Make certain to praise your self each time you gain this type of desires.

The maximum crucial detail that you may do is to create a plan that works properly for you. There are such some of plans and applications to be had that declare they may art work for each person. However, the reality is those programs were not created for you. These applications were created thru someone who found a software program software that worked well for them. No one is aware of you better than you do because of this that which you are the simplest individual who can create a software at the way to paintings properly for you.

This way which you do no longer push yourself too hard, which you do no longer try to compete with the ones round you, and that you hobby on getting to know English and pleasant studying English.

Spend some time thinking about the techniques that have worked properly for you inside the beyond, then regulate the ones strategies to ensure that they may paintings well for you presently and within the destiny.

Learn English Phrases

One of the maximum critical steps of mastering English fluently is to investigate English phrases. The reason for this is due to the truth if you most effective attention on learning one word at a time, while you try to sincerely talk in English, it is going to take some of questioning that allows you to string words collectively and form sentences. This honestly takes an excessive amount of paintings. However, in case you interest on studying terms, you may be prepared with responses regardless of what situation you find yourself in. You will need to suppose an awful lot less, and your English will encounter as greater herbal.

A top notch manner to discover ways to use not unusual phrases is to locate a person online who you could talk with every day. You do now not must spend an hour each day talking on your English speakme friend on-line asking that they assist you apprehend what sure terms endorse. Make fantastic you've got a plan for the time that the two of you spend on line, or you could discover that you get off situation matter and do now not attain your dreams. If there's no English speakme buddy available, you can lease someone to help you studies English via chatting on the diverse freelance websites.

You can also discover someone to speak with on what is known as a conversation exchange internet website on-line. On this kind of net web page, you can find out someone who desires to observe your local language and is inclined to help you have a have a look at theirs. In order to do that, you may want to spend half of of of the time you communicate in conjunction with your companion speakme in your native language and the alternative half of of in their neighborhood language.

While you are analyzing those terms, you need to apprehend that your primary cause of analyzing English is with a view to talk with those round you. This approach which you do now not need to fear approximately using right grammar while you're first stringing terms together. However, even as you emerge as more fluent, you can reputation on grammar.

While you are getting to know how to mention those phrases– we are able to go over maximum of the most commonplace terms of the English language in the subsequent bankruptcy– make sure that you communicate slowly and virtually. Many exceptional languages are spoken right away. However, the English language is spoken slowly, and if you communicate too fast, your words will not be understood.

You might also moreover find out that inside the middle of a phrase, you forget about the phrase that you were going to use. If this takes place, it's far k, and it's miles not anything to get too worried about. Simply seek your mind for some different word to fill the void within the sentence. Try now not to get too creative, and when you have to ask for help from the person who you're talking too, do not revel in ashamed.

No count number quantity what you consider your English, in no manner begin a sentence out thru the usage of apologizing in your ability degree. No one is going to count on that you speak first-class English, and you could simply wonder them at how proper you may communicate.

While it's far essential which will have a examine the meanings of terms that you are going to use, in case you need to begin speaking English fluently and rapid, you want to discover ways to memorize exclusive phrases.

There are numerous techniques with a view to memorize terms, and any such is to pick one word for the day. Let's say for instance, "My name is Phillip." This is a phrase that you'll use all the time, each single day, and it's far one that you want to have the potential to say without making any mistakes. Write the word on an index card and read it out loud 3 or 4 times inside the morning. Read it once more a few instances after lunch, try remembering it inside the route of the day, and repeat it yet again a few greater times earlier than you visit mattress.

The next day, you will upload some other card with some different phrase, and on the same time as education the second phrase, you may refresh your thoughts through reading the primary phrase out loud that day. After this you may hold to feature playing cards, reviewing the preceding gambling playing cards each day, ensuring that you maintain in mind any of the phrases.

You can also make the terms into a tune that will help you hold in thoughts them. Simply create a chunk music, the usage of the beat of your preferred song and make the phrases the latest lyrics.

If you encounter a word that you are having a tough time remembering, together with "petrified," you can destroy the phrase down so you can recall it better, together with PETeR IF he dIED. This explains the phrase petrified at the same time as reminding you of the manner to say the word. You see, Peter if he died is probably petrified.

If you are attempting to analyze phrases that you already understand, but in a particular collection that makes the word, you'll have to spend hundreds of time working closer to.

However, I need to move over some precise phrases for you to analyze at the manner to be of assist to you as you're studying to talk higher English.

- Can you help me?

- I want instructions.

- A long term in the beyond.

- Am I saying this efficaciously?

- Do you need assist?

- Are you doing anything this night?

- I am hungry.

- Are you hungry?

- Is the whole thing adequate?

- Do you feel sick?

- Are you fine?

- What time?

- Can you translate this?

- Be very careful.

- Don't fear.

- How are you?

- I can't pay attention it.

- I can't pay interest you.

- I don't understand how.

- I don't like him.

- I want to transport domestic.

- Let me recognise if you need a few help.

- I need to get to this deal with.

- I'll see you tomorrow.

- I'll goodbye.

- You are very pretty.

- Thank you for assisting me.

- Can I depart a message?

Learning the ones phrases goes to help get you started out out talking English fluently. It is going to make sure that you're going on the manner to communicate with the ones which you want to speak with. These phrases are going to help you get in which you want to move, allow a person apprehend which you are interested in them or that you want assist. These are the maximum important terms in an attempt to investigate and understand.

Build Your Vocabulary

There are many strategies for you to build up your vocabulary so that you are a higher English speaker. The first detail that you need to do, but, is to make a dedication to learning new English terms on a regular basis.

It does not depend if you need to have a look at a today's word every day or a brand new phrase each week, as long as you make a decision to mastering new terms, you may watch your vocabulary amplify dramatically.

By growing your vocabulary, you can make certain that you are able to speak better, sound more like a local English speaker, and show human beings which you are an clever individual. Learning new terms can also moreover even be amusing, and you could assignment a chum to take a look at the words with you.

In this economic catastrophe, I want to teach you the way you can build up your vocabulary and studies new phrases so that you are in a position to speak higher and sound like a nearby English speaker.

Read every single day, as a bargain as possible. The top notch way a excellent manner to growth your vocabulary is to have a take a look at pretty some books written in English and take the time to look up phrases which you do now not understand. The extra phrases you are uncovered to on a every day foundation, the extra phrases you'll have a look at and recognize.

Make effective that you maintain a dictionary with you always. When you are analyzing, it's miles essential an amazing manner to have a dictionary so you can look up the phrases which you do now not recognize. However, it's also crucial so that you can maintain one nearby at the identical time as you are looking tv or paying attention to a podcast. This will make certain that you may pause the display, appearance up the phrase that you do no longer apprehend or understand, and research it. This will now not first-rate can help you increase your vocabulary, however it'll moreover make sure that you understand what goes on within the show.

Keep a word mag. This goes to be one in every of a kind than a everyday journal. It goes to be a mag or strolling listing of the words that you have found out. This will ensure that you are capable of look once more over the terms that you have found out making sure that you recollect any of them. When you look at a brand new word, certainly write it to your phrase magazine at the side of the definition. Once each week you should cross over the phrases, the usage of each one in a sentence. If you find out that you are having a difficult time with one word, spend a while education it until you completely recognize a way to use it.

Spend a while gambling phrase video video games. This is a super way to extend your vocabulary. There are many online video games that you can play on my own or you can play Scrabble together along with your pals. Games that require you to find out phrases which can be indexed in a puzzle are notable if you are simply beginning out with reference to growing your vocabulary. Games like Scrabble are tremendous for preserving new phrases glowing in your mind.

Spend a while talking to awesome people. Just talking with exceptional humans will reveal you to new terms. You is probably exposed to excellent slang phrases, fillers, and terms relying on wherein the person is from, what they do for a living, and wherein they grew up. When you hear a person say a word that you do now not recognize, jot it down in a small pocket ebook so you can appearance it up later. After you recognize what the word way, you may upload it to your vocabulary by means of way of slowly beginning to apply it on your each day conversations.

You are in charge of your very very personal vocabulary. It is as much as you to take rate and make a willpower to increasing it; analyzing new phrases on a regular foundation. When you popularity on growing your vocabulary, you may no longer first-rate amplify your records of the English language, however you are also going to make certain that you sound extra like a community English speaker.

Most importantly, you want to consider to workout the cutting-edge phrases which you study each unmarried day, or you will lose the phrases. If you do no longer exercise some thing that you are trying to study, you will now not be capable of keep it for your brain. This manner which you want to commit time every day to going for walks for your vocabulary.

Practice Makes Perfect

Practice makes perfect irrespective of what you are trying to have a look at and that includes the English language as well. In this bankruptcy, I need to offer you some techniques if you want to exercise to enhance your English language fluency.

Start a e-book membership together together together with your friends. It is a top notch idea if you need to begin a ebook club, preferably with as a minimum one local English speaker. This will make sure that if you have any questions, you can have someone to ask, someone who will offer an motive behind to you the that means of terms, terms, and sentences. Make sure that you are reading cutting-edge books. It is quite tough for many community English audio device to understand a number of the older romance novels and also you ought to not attempt to carry out that until you're fluent in the English language. A film club is also an remarkable idea. You can spend one night time time time ordinary with week searching a film after which discussing it in conjunction with your organization. Talk approximately the different factors of the film, the new phrases which you discovered in addition to what you did not understand.

Offer to assist precise humans in exchange for his or her assist. Perhaps you can offer to assist translate at artwork, or in all likelihood you could offer to assist someone research your local language in the event that they might assist you take a look at English.

Practice repeating a communication in one among your chosen movies. Have you ever positioned it extraordinary that humans can imitate their favored characters? The way that they do this is that they spend quite a few time looking the man or woman and repeating what the person has stated. Listen to a sentence that your favored character has said, pause the display, repeat what they stated, attempting your awesome to pronounce it much like the man or woman at the show. After you have got were given have been given finished this, be aware of what the alternative person says and repeat the manner, saying the second individual's terms. This will make certain that you do not stroll round sounding like you're imitating a selected individual, but it's going to make sure that you could spend some time focusing on how you're pronouncing the phrases.

Find an internet instruct, one who is inclined to Skype with you on a regular foundation. Often, if you provide to teach the man or woman your nearby language, they will help you find out how to speak theirs. This is likewise a excellent manner on the way to make new pals everywhere inside the united states of america or perhaps the arena.

You can, of course, take some English instructions. However, this can get pretty expensive. This is a remarkable choice when you have the cash for it; if not, you may use the loose commands that you could find on YouTube. If you discern for a company that goals you to improve upon your English, possibilities are, you can get them to pay for the instructions.

Make it a dependancy of questioning earlier than you speak. When someone asks you a question, take some moments and take into account what your reaction can be. Even folks who communicate English as their first language need to take some time to hold in thoughts what they're going to mention in advance than they'll be announcing it. Practice having conversations at the same time as you are inside the shower or even as you are by myself. Focus on announcing your phrases properly.

Practice is essential in case you need to reap fulfillment at talking English fluently. It is some aspect that want to be completed on a every day basis. You ought to do it every day of the week, along with at the weekends. You ought to ensure that you are spending as an awful lot of your unfastened time as you likely can practicing the English language.

Learn English Grammar

When you first start talking English fluently, you want to focus at the terms, phrases, and pronunciation. However, as time passes, you'll want to spend some time specializing in grammar.

You may also need to enhance your grammar because of instructional motives, for personal motives or for professional reasons. You may also furthermore clearly want to enhance your grammar because of the truth you want to appear more like a neighborhood English speaker.

In order to get started out out, it's miles crucial so that it will ask yourself why you need to decorate your grammar. Perhaps you need to enhance your professional life, write higher, or make better grades. Everyone is going to have a unique purpose for trying to enhance their grammar, however a training path is useful because it will awareness at the truth that you aren't a community speaker.

The first component that you have to do is to spend an entire lot of time studying. While you're reading, you want to interest at the grammar in every and each sentence. For example, as you are reading thru this book, you have to take word of wherein commas and apostrophes are located. Focus on all the punctuation. Grammar focuses on the whole form of the language, not just the phrases spoken or the punctuation so which means that you need to take be aware about each a part of every sentence.

Many humans have a difficult time studying English grammar, but it isn't as hard as many human beings try and make it.

Another wonderful way that permits you to discover ways to accurate your grammar is to down load a software program, which includes Ginger or Grammarly. These will display up as add-ons for your Word utility and could assist you learn how to use better grammar whilst you are writing. In order to use the ones, you'll need to workout writing to your computer each day; even though it is only some hundred phrases, this is going to ensure which you learn from your errors. Grammarly is a outstanding application to use even as doing this due to the fact even as this device famous errors, it explains them to you.

If you need to spend a while exciting, down load a grammar app or game for your tablet or pc; even as you are playing the sport, you will be enhancing your grammar competencies.

Make excellent that you pay attention to the mistakes that you generally make and focus on now not repeating them again. If you recognize that you are growing a mistake, as an example, using its in region of it's, in reality know-how approximately the mistake isn't always sufficient, you have to make the effort to correct it as well.

There are many free grammar packages on line that you can use, and that is the excellent factor that you could do if you really need to beautify your grammar.

Chapter 7: Exploring Your Own Voice

The human voice is a big part of who we are and the way we carry out inside the society. You convey your voice everywhere your bypass; you can't honestly leave it at domestic not like your telephones or your wallets (which you need to not leave at home as nicely, but that is already a one in every of a type story). And in advance than we even start studying a manner to growth an top notch speakme capability, it's far crucial that we find out our non-public voice first.

Our voice is a totally powerful and vital tool that we've were given for it tells other humans plenty of factors approximately you. It also impacts the way human beings apprehend and create impressions approximately you.

Experts genuinely keep in mind the human voice as a person's "calling card." They say that the voice speaks for yourself greater than your garments or your bodily appearance do. Once humans listen your voice, they mechanically create assumptions about you based totally on what they've got honestly heard.

Most people moreover typically generally tend to determine you based totally mostly on the way you talk to them, or essentially on the manner you talk. There are a few who think that someone isn't always authoritative sufficient because his or her voice seems to be so gentle, even though the case may be in any other case. There also are some times in which someone thinks of a person else as impolite or disrespectful just due to the reality what she or he has sincerely said. So reputedly, your voice in addition to the way you communicate tells exclusive humans lots approximately your self.

Poet Henry Longfellow once stated that "the human voice is the organ of the soul." How you'll be capable of encourage and encourage outstanding humans may additionally moreover depend upon the manner you talk to others. You can also circulate them and have an effect on their viewpoints in existence honestly thru using the way you communicate to them in addition to through the use of the topics which you say to them.

Judy Apps, an international voice professional similarly to an creator of a few books approximately talking, counseled the following issues on how the electricity of your voice can change the way people endure in thoughts you, each via manner of way of lifting them up or setting them down:

•As a manager, you may both make the human beings at your work recognize your beneficial resource or intimidate them without a doubt thru the manner you speak to them.

•As a caregiver, you may both deliver the humans you cope with peace of mind and make them experience higher or upload strain to them.

•As a hard and fast leader, you can every encourage further to energise your human beings to art work extra hard and take a look at you, or you could discourage them to go on.

•As a decide or a parent, you may both inspire your kids to try tougher to gain their dreams in existence or demotivate them to reach all their potentials.

•As a teacher, you may both beautify your pupil's self warranty in his or herself or put off all their self-respect and self-esteem.

•As a educate, you could each inspire different people to reflect on themselves and speak to them to motion, or purpose them to count on which you are being oppressive and take their self perception away.

"Voice is an fundamental part of the whole message," says Apps. Our voice is answerable for giving life and due to this to the entirety we're announcing. If you communicate with a expert and confident voice, then humans will most in all likelihood take you as a professional and even take you significantly.

Let us admit, in spite of the fact that, that not anybody is gifted with an super speaking potential. There are times whilst you without a doubt can't communicate the way you want to. Regardless how frequently you need to sound authoritative, you clearly can't because of the fact your voice is so clean and calm. You get the point.

Also, the ones folks that are assured enough to speak in public most of the time get greater opportunities than people who are not that assured. Even former United States Secretary Colin Powell as soon as admitted in his autobiography that having the ability to speak in public effects and early in his existence made a massive impact on his achievement. He became even promoted in art work due to the fact he has properly talking competencies.

However, it does not necessarily recommend that most effective the ones parents which can be actual in talking get to collect existence. After all, now not all accurate audio system are proper because of the truth they were born; a few are honed through exercising. I the subsequent chapters, we're in a position to speak the techniques on how you can beautify your voice in phrases of your talking abilities.

Chapter 8: Why Decorate Speakme Abilties

Imagine an afternoon even as all of a unexpected you may not communicate. Imagine being a scenario wherein you really need to mention something but people won't certainly pay attention to you. Imagine your self being in an area in which no person pay attention to you regardless how crucial the property you're speaking approximately. Wouldn't that be the one of the worst subjects ever?

Just like what we've got have been given said in the preceding financial ruin, having the capability to talk nicely and efficaciously can provide you with some of possibilities. People will take you significantly and preserve in thoughts you as a professional in case you communicate optimistically with the voice of a professional. So it's miles crucial that you increase the skill in talking with reference to what you need to be (or possibly, sound like).

Judy Apps moreover referred to some advantages of getting the potential to speak well, now not without a doubt in the the the front of a large target marketplace, however even truely to the small enterprise of people that you stumble upon to your regular existence. Aside from the fact that once your voice speaks properly for you, you create a high-quality verbal exchange and interaction with unique human beings, proper here are some blessings of having an super speaking capability.

1. Being understood really. Basically, at the identical time as you communicate properly, humans may be able to recognize you better and genuinely. When you speak very speedy, then humans will not understand a unmarried word which you say. Also, if you talk properly, human beings should have a higher understanding of the message that you need to impose. For instance, in case you mumble, human beings will have the impression that you could no longer need to

be there. It also can appear to them that you do now not need to speak to them so you are without a doubt mumbling in area of creating them pay interest what you're absolutely pronouncing. But at the same time as you speak without a doubt, human beings will be aware of you and they may genuinely recognize the matters that you are speaking approximately.

2. Being a delight to concentrate to. Isn't it precise to recognize that people revel in paying attention to the subjects that you are talking about? Keep in mind that powerful conversation moreover is based upon on whether or not the aim marketplace is taking note of you or no longer. People will not concentrate to you inside the occasion that they do not revel in the revel in of taking note of you. If you sound anxious, then people will most probably anticipate that you aren't organized in turning in your speech. People will suppose which you are not a first rate talking, therefore taking you

as dull. As a forestall end result, they may lose interest to what you are saying, and you will not be able to talk properly with them.

3. Being extra confident. If in yourself that you are an first rate speaker, then you may most probable increase that self guarantee every time you have have been given to speak in the the front of different human beings. If you increase an tremendous speaking knowledge, then you may boom self guarantee as nicely. Speaking nicely ensures you that you could not fail due to the reality you are prepared to perform that and also you recognize what you are doing. This in flip will make you extra assured to talk up and interact more humans to take note of you.

4. Being capable of deliver authority. When you speak with a steadier voice because of this authority, human beings will in turn take you notably, thinking that you have an professional over them. Moreover, at the

equal time as you are the chief in your university or in your paintings, your humans will then take into account which you have authority over them due to the reality you communicate authoritatively.

5. Being able to entertain human beings. Speaking properly can sooner or later entertain your goal market and maintain their interest for your speech. Always maintain in thoughts that attractive your target market is sincerely taken into consideration one in all your goals even as speaking. It makes you keep in mind your listeners and the manner you may be able to keep them interested by what you're announcing as an alternative on simply that specialize in how authentic or bad your typical performance can be. Basically, real speaking abilities help in giving your speech a selection in phrases of the situation depend range, amount, pace, tone, and others. It moreover gives you spontaneity, humor, amusement in addition to

recollections or anecdotes as you deliver your speech.

6. Being able to construct rapport.

In communique, it's miles very essential which you keep related collectively along with your goal marketplace. Always keep in thoughts that it's far crucial which you apprehend your goal market and you build rapport with them. Good speakme skills will in flip interact your target market to pay attention to you. You can be capable of construct ideal relationships with them thru effective verbal exchange.

How to decorate your speakme abilties

Have you ever felt so apprehensive on every occasion you have got were given got to speak within the front of humans? Have you ever had your knees and arms shake every time you are reputation in the the front of your goal marketplace? Do not fear; it is not the give up of the arena for you!

There will continually come a time on your lifestyles in which you want to growth your boundaries. There may be a time wherein you need to bypass from talking to simply one precise person, permit us to mention your pal or your discern, to addressing a huge corporation of people, allow us to mention your complete classmate in your lecture beauty or the humans to your work group. The concept is that talking to the overall public aim marketplace is inevitable.

But within the first area, why are we terrified of speakme in public?

It may be due to the fact we assume that human beings could not care much less approximately what we are going to talk about. We experience like as quickly as we start speakme, they may genuinely be yawning and be organized to be able to stop your speech as a way to have their freedom. Or maybe you had a disturbing revel in in the past in which you had been humiliated on the identical time as talking in the the front of human beings.

However, those need to not restrict you from speaking your self up. Now is the perfect time at the manner to understand how you may be capable of beautify your competencies in talking and knock all your fears away.

In this financial ruin, we are able to communicate about the techniques on how you'll be capable of decorate your speakme skills. We may also even very well speak how you will be able to knock your worry of speaking in public after which talk your self up with a view to have better possibilities in your career and in your lifestyles.

Chapter 9: Knock Your Worry Down

We recognize that your biggest enemywith regards to talking is worry. And while you worry, you hesitate.

Basically, you hesitate every time you communicate within the the front of an goal marketplace due to the fact you are not so sure about what you are going to say subsequent. You can also start thinking that you are going to fail when you speak about this specific recall. You moreover revel in like your target audience do not care approximately what you're talking approximately.

Usually, it is apparent which you are hesitating, or worried in desired, at the same time as you are frequently saying "um" or "er" or different fillers that are not vital on your speech. Also, your audience may also additionally moreover discover the ones fillers disturbing and they may not be aware of you. You may also be tripping over your very own phrases from time to time because you are dashing to particular your ideas as your thoughts works quicker than your lips. Most of the time, speakme quicker implies that you are concerned.

For you in order to knock your hesitations, maintain in mind the subsequent steps:

•Think greater definitely. Doing this will help you hobby on an appropriate recollect which you are speaking approximately, in an effort to in flip make you talk in reality and nicely.

•Slow down and emphasize your factors. It isn't always properly to speak fast and come upon your terms; this could only make your speech difficult to understand. It is also essential which you emphasize your key elements in order that your goal market will understand in which your speech is leading. This can even help you live focused.

•Breathe well. Proper respiratory permits you stay comfortable. This may additionally keep you speak well in order that your goal marketplace can be capable of recognize you well.

When it entails handling your anxiety, maintain in mind the following hints:

•Do not make your nerves avoid you. Do now not always interest on your self. Think approximately special audio machine getting fearful too! But that isn't the entire factor. Just hold in mind as nicely that the human beings you're speaking to isn't always that aware of how worried you're. There was a announcing as quickly as that is going like this: "It is best to have butterflies—as long as they fly in formation."

•Connect collectively together with your target audience. The fulfillment of each communique drift is primarily based upon at the effects of it to the intended target market. Therefore, because the speaker, it's far critical that you understand the people that you are going to speak to and also you hook up with them. Make sure that you understand their cutting-edge-day mood as you communicate. If they're bored, make certain that you are active to shape of wake them up.

•Have your goals in your mind. It is important that you recognize why you're speakme. Giving speeches is not only approximately disseminating statistics; it is also approximately attractive your target audience and giving them what they need. Always preserve in thoughts your desires or the cause why you are talking. Do you want to entertain people? Do you need to inform or probable educate them?

•Be immoderate best. Always consider succeeding. Imagine yourself speaking with a chunk of success and actually. Paint a picture of yourself speakme without any flaws or mistakes. Always hobby your thoughts on your preferred very last effects—the matters which you need to reap and now not the matters that you do not like.

•Relax. Again, it's far critical which you stay snug even as you are speaking. Remove all of the tensions, hesitations, and some thing apprehensive for your device as you speak. Tell your self with a grin which you are suitable sufficient.

Speak up!

Judy Apps has also listed ten methods on you may have the capability to speak with authority similarly to with air of thriller. Here's how:

When become the ultimate time you heard someone talk with authority? With air of secrecy? How did you revel in whilst you've got been listening? Did you enjoy like he or she is a very credible character, with power and affect?

Speaking nicely is probably one of the most common matters that we want to gain. We need to sound authoritative genuinely so humans will take us as confident and credible audio device. This can also make your target market pay extra interest to you and to what you are speakme approximately because of the truth they discover you influential and effective.

Here are Apps' hints on how you may be capable of enhance your speakme talents:

1. Stand with self belief.

Basically, the way you stand additionally affects how you speak. If you stand with a piece of good fortune, then you can maximum in all likelihood have the potential to talk with a bit of luck as well. People may also understand you as assured when you consider that they are able to see you reputation with poise, therefore they will provide you with their interest. Standing nicely may additionally help you produce a better sound or voice at the same time as talking.

You can enhance your posture as you communicate with the useful resource of locating your balance. Have your weight distributed flippantly amongst your ft so that you will no longer stumble. Stand tall as nicely and preserve your chin lifted up. Doing so moreover offers for your top without any efforts.

Moreover, you moreover mght want to lighten up (how typically have we already emphasised this trouble in this ebook? Oh properly) and breathe. Release all the anxiety for your face, jaw, neck, and shoulders. Breathe out as properly and permit the air make bigger your complete frame.

2. Speak in reality.

If you speak absolutely and audibly, you could sound as if you truly suggest what you're pronouncing. It will sound like what you are saying comes from your coronary coronary coronary heart. This may even help you've got interplay your audience to pay attention to you due to the truth they recognize what you're saying.

Open your mouth nicely as you talk, despite the fact that you aren't that used to it. This can also sense uncomfortable inside the beginning, but it may also come herbal for your target marketplace. Practice the mouth exercise as well. Make the vowel sounds greater distinguishable and your consonants clearer as well.

3. Project nicely.

Judy Apps indicates that humans will maximum probable take you significantly in case your voice has an impact to them. Therefore, it's miles critical that you mission your voice in step with the message which you want to impose for your audience.

four. Give emphasis in your key factors.

For you as a way to deliver your message to your purpose marketplace virtually and effectively, it's far critical that you emphasize your key factors. This will allow the your goal market understand what are the vital factors of your speech and deliver hobby to you as you speak approximately those points. Also, there are instances at the same time as unique audio device deliver equal emphasis on each a part of their speech, therefore making it seem monotonous and stupid. The sound very flat, which in flip makes the listeners bored and experience sleepy. If you need to sound authoritative and charismatic, you need to emphasise strongly.

5. Do not rush.

How rapid or sluggish you communicate might also have an effect on the have an effect on you're making amongst distinct humans. If you communicate very speedy, it is able to seem like you're excited speaking about that particular problem depend. People may also assume that you do not need to speak to them due to the truth you're rushing topics. On the opposite hand, in case you speak slowly, people might imagine of you as stupid and they'll subsequently get tired listening to you.

The factor is that you need to expose the price of your speech. You neither have to speak fast or slowly; you need to keep it cautiously. Your velocity may also variety, counting on what you are pronouncing and the message you want to give for your target market. Again, you want to emphasise essential elements, so that you have to not supply identical weight and tempo to each a part of your communicate.

6. Use your instruments.

We are gifted with exquisite gadgets. It just is based upon on how we are going to use them to have the ability to speak properly.

Make your tone tough or clean, counting on what you want to say. You can also want to extend your vowels and use them to specific feelings. On the opportunity hand, use consonants without difficulty or sharply to make your speech clearer.

You should moreover range your pitch; preserve your voice excessive or deep or everywhere in among, relying for your message. Use notable volumes as properly in which you have got to speak loudly in some a part of your speech and softly in others. There are also some elements in which you have to talk speedy or slowly, relying on the elements you need to emphasize.

7. Practice, exercising, and practice.

If you are having a hard time pronouncing a specific word, then exercising it virtually so the following time you've got to say it, you couldn't have a hassle with it. Make great that you also workout your modulation, articulation, and something else that has a few element to do with talking.

It is likewise crucial that you communicate fluently. You want to suppose in reality and recognize what you are going to say subsequent. Again, you genuinely start to hesitate even as speakme due to the fact you're taking location to be uncertain approximately what you will do and say subsequent. If you may do a huge speech approximately a specific venture recall, it's miles crucial which you do your studies first to widen your information about that project recall. Then write your personal speech so you realise thoroughly how it'll move. And then exercising turning in that speech for as a first rate deal time as critical.

Again, because of the reality the announcing is going, "Practice makes best."

8. Just be first rate all of the time.

There is not any man or woman else that permit you to however your self. If you don't forget your self succeeding, then you could maximum likely act towards reaching achievement. Do no longer bombard your mind with the thoughts that you are going to fail, because of the truth you are not. You will be triumphant if you are determined sufficient that you'll be triumphant!

Chapter 10: Abomination

— A person or element this is disgusting and frequently substantially despised. How do you practice this word? You use this phrase whilst you want to speak about a few detail this is disgusting, offensive and hated. Some say the manner he disciplines his kids want to be considered an abomination.

abstain

— One who voluntarily chooses no longer to do something or revel in some aspect. How do you study this phrase? You use this word at the equal time as you speak about a few element you choose no longer to do. Michael abstained from his usually immoderate eating on Fridays.

absurd

— Ridiculously irrational, unreasonable or illogical. How do you examine this phrase? You use this word to describe some thing this is glaringly fake or untrue. He regarded to have the absurd idea that during case you bang it more tough, it's going to begin jogging over again.

accommodate

— To do a kindness for, offer for, deliver or lend coins to. How do you workout this phrase? You use this phrase on the identical time as you're speakme about someone or some thing who gives for or resources for. The inn we have been staying at emerge as more accommodating then the closing motels we stayed at.

responsible

— Required to report, deliver an explanation for or justify some thing. How do you apply this phrase? You use this phrase whilst you need to give an explanation for some thing or someone who is liable for a selected movement. Paul modified into held accountable for the selection that he made to buy greater stocks.

widely recognized

— To understand the lifestyles, fact or fact of. How do you observe this word? You use this word whilst you want to speak approximately recognizing the truth of some factor. He noted the truth that education can be very critical and crucial.

adamant

— Unyielding, impervious to being persuaded, pleas, motive or common revel in. How do you practice this word? You use this phrase at the identical time as you need to give an explanation for someone who stubbornly refuses to be persuaded and trade their mind or something unbreakable or impenetrable. Steve modified into adamant about his opinion that Chinese food is higher than Japanese food.

adept

— Very expert. How do you practice this phrase? You use this phrase whilst you are describing someone who is very proficient at some trouble or mainly professional. The darkish sorcerer have turn out to be scarily adept at effective black magic.

adequate

— Enough to fulfill a name for or need without being plentiful. How do you observe this phrase? You use this phrase while you show that something is enough to fulfill a need. Paul packed an acceptable sufficient quantity of meals for the tenting enjoy.

adore

— The act of loving and respecting someone or something. How do you test this phrase? You use this phrase even as you want to depict the most love and admiration for some thing or a person. Peter may be very captivated with technology and adores what each detail of it is able to produce.

adversity

— Difficulties or misfortune. How do you exercising this phrase? You use this phrase to talk about the problems of some thing.

Rachel come to be going via a massive quantity of adversity from her family due to her divorce.

suggest

– To communicate, plead or argue for a cause; a supporter of a few thing. How do you follow this phrase? You use this phrase to provide an reason behind a person who defends or speaks for a motive. Sally is an suggest for justice and equality inside the u.S. She lives in.

affinity

– A robust, natural liking or attraction for a few element or a person. How do you take a look at this phrase? You use this word to explain a effective enchantment or liking for some thing or a person.

She acquired a robust affinity to Celine Dion and Madonna songs the instantaneous she heard them.

worry

– To go through severe pain or to go through super intellectual warfare. How do you exercising this phrase? You use this phrase whilst you're speakme about struggling pain or ache over something. The preference of white or wheat bread for a sandwich is not some thing to worry about.

alienate

– To come to be withdrawn or isolated and to shy away because of hostility or anger. How do you exercise this phrase? You use this phrase whilst you are talking approximately some thing who has located himself/herself as a distance from those who cared but no longer. Ryan's drug dependancy added about discomfort for his own family and friends which ended up with him being alienated.

align

– To satisfactory friend with one aspect of a motive or argument or to get someone, vicinity or element proper right into a at once line. How do you observe this word? You use this word to speak about someone who sided with a specific reason or to vicinity a few element in a proper away line. He selected to align himself with like-minded those who keep in mind in freedom.

alleviate

— To make a few issue simpler to deal with or reduce the pain of something. How do you comply with this word? You use this word whilst you're talking about some component that comforts, decreases pain or makes something less tough to address. His doctor prescribed a unique ache-killer to relieve his sprain.

allude

— To hint at now not immediately however not bypass into detail. How do you test this phrase? You use this word even as you're talking approximately some thing you or someone else isn't at once hinting at. All of his factors seem to allude to the same stop.

modify

— Changing or making a few aspect awesome. How do you exercise this phrase? You use this phrase even as you are describing or depicting a trade or adjustment. Monica desired to regulate her face with the aid of the usage of getting plastic surgery.

ambidextrous

— Capable of using every hands effortlessly. How do you study this phrase? You use this word at the identical time as you are describing a person who is succesful to make use of each hands effectively. You have a positive benefit over specific artist in case you are ambidextrous.

ambiguous

— Something that is dubious or capable of being interpreted in or extra strategies. How do you follow this phrase? You use this phrase on the identical time as you speak about a few component which could suggest or be interpreted in or more approaches.   Steve's   observation approximately abortion became ambiguous.

ambitious

— Full of motivation and preference or requiring lots attempt. How do you study this word? You use this word to describe some problem this is difficult and appropriate or someone who drastically goals fulfillment. He proved to be very ambitious collectively together with his picture layout paintings.

amend

— To change and get rid of the faults and errors for the higher or to decorate. How do you exercise this phrase? You use this phrase while you are speakme approximately a few issue that alters and modifies for the better. His apology to his girlfriend amended their dating.

enough

– An abundance or sufficient of a few issue to meet a need or reason. How do you look at this word? You use this phrase to mention you have have been given an abundance of some thing with some left over. The charity accumulated an enough quantity of donations for optimum cancers studies.

animosity

– A powerful, adverse feeling or dislike. How do you exercise this phrase? You use this word to describe a strong feeling of resentment or hatred. Sue had animosity within the direction of Greg based totally absolutely completely on the gossip she had heard about him.

antic

– An hobby-getting, funny, and playful act, gesture or posture. How do you have a look at this phrase? You use this phrase to categorize any playful or humorous act, trick, prank, gesture or posture. Trevor's antics were given him in intense problem collectively together with his mother and father and the law.

apostate

– Someone who discards their non secular religion, a political business corporation employer, requirements or motive. How do you follow this phrase? You use this phrase to describe someone who leaves their religion or cause. He have come to be deemed an apostate, and those knew whilst he stopped going to church and taking part in Bible have a have a have a look at.

attraction

– To make an excessive or honest request, as for help or the power to attract or amuse. How do you study this phrase? You use this phrase while you want to speak about a request for help or useful aid or to provide a request to a person or authority for a desire.

The committee failed to look to kindly at his enchantment to prohibit positive humans from the enterprise.

relevant

— Something this is suitable or relevant and capable of be finished. How do you observe this phrase? You use this word on the identical time as you are speakme approximately some component that can or can not be truly used for something applicable. It is not applicable to apply a screwdriver to check the oil of your car.

apprehension

— The nation of being disturbing after the anticipation of some thing lousy. How do you practice this phrase? You use this phrase to speak approximately the sensation of anxiety or fear over what also can display up. He didn't muster sufficient self belief to method the lovely lady because of his apprehension.

arbitrary

— Based on private feelings or person judgment in preference to motive, commonplace sense or regulation. How do you workout this phrase? You use this word while you come across mind, reviews or mind which can be primarily based on private opportunities. The customers did not just like the immoderate, arbitrary prices of the CD gamers.

arcane

— Secret and mysterious; understood thru only a few. How do you examine this phrase? Whenever you want to explain a few problem it is mysterious that only some humans understand. Maxwell's records of scared voodoo magic emerge as arcane to maximum of the wizard's of his day.

articulate

— To speak or specific your self effortlessly, in truth and fluently; to speak efficiently.

How do you have a examine this word? You use this phrase at the same time as you want to explain a person who's speakme and expressing themselves. Charles seemed to have problem articulating why he thinks Edgar Allan Poe is better than Robert Frost.

affirm

— To discover, discover or study with truth by using the use of examination or experimentation. How do you workout this word? You use this phrase on the same time as you are talking about some thing this is found with truth and observed out from research. Supernatural findings or evaluations may be difficult to look at.

asinine

— Very silly, foolish or stupid. How do you look at this word? You use this phrase whilst you're describing a few component very unintelligent or stupid. Robert's concept is may be humorous to play in site visitors but it turn out to be simply asinine.

aspiration

– Having a robust desire or an ambitious purpose. How do you follow this word? You use this phrase to explain inspiring achievements or goals. Micheal's aspirations for his writing profession end up extraordinary and certainly high.

assert

– To proclaim with self perception and to defend. How do you exercise this phrase? You use this phrase whilst you, a person or a few difficulty is setting fourth a declaration or opinion about some aspect with self perception. Leonard asserted that the earth rotates throughout the sun.

atheist

– One who has a disbelief within the existence of a God or gods. How do you observe this word? You use this word to explain a person who does now not obtain as real with in a supernatural deity or God.

When Sarah asked me to go to church, I informed her I modified into an atheist.

achieve

— To advantage, attain or accomplish with attempt. How do you exercise this phrase? You use this phrase even as you're speaking approximately something you obtained or received because of a few labor or attempt. Level 50 is the extremely good level you may collect.

audacity

— Fearlessness or competitive boldness specially with self notion and arrogance. How do you workout this word? You use this word to provide an explanation for a person or some thing, who is movements are fearless and arrogantly formidable. Jose had the audacity to insult a random stranger, for no reason.

babble

– To talk a meaningless confusion of phrases in a foolish or excited manner. How do you examine this phrase? You use this phrase at the same time as someone is appearing to be speaking a package deal of meaningless, incoherent jumble of phrases. He changed into angry and having a tough time attempting to speak. It might probable of sounded satisfactory to him however to anyone else it became babble.

baffle

– To confuse or to puzzle. How do you exercise this word? You use this phrase whilst you are describing a few element this is difficult and hard to recognize. The magic trick the magician showed the children changed into so suitable, it even baffled most of the adults!

ballistic

– To grow to be very angry or violently enraged. How do you follow this word? You use this word to give an explanation for the feeling of unexpected anger or excitement. He went ballistic after locating out he received a five hundred dollar rate ticket.

bane

— The cause of exceptional distress, damage or break. How do you test this phrase? You use this phrase while you're speaking about some factor that motives top notch annoyance or ruins. Excessive playing and wastefulness modified into the bane of his finances.

banter

— To speak to in a playful, great or teasing manner. How do you examine this phrase? You use this word at the same time as you're describing teasing comments which might be made in a playful way. Calvin bantered with nearly everyone at his party.

bare

— Exposed to view or no longer hid; naked or nude. How do you apply this word? You use this phrase to provide an explanation for some issue this is exposed or bare. He become left undergo, sitting within the clinical medical doctors place of business.

barrage

— An overwhelming amount or explosion of some aspect in conjunction with terms, criticism, opinions, questions, and so forth. How do you practice this word? You use this phrase to explain the delivery of a large amount of a few element. After giving his opinion, he received a barrage of criticism and accusations.

befriend

— To end up or behave as a friend to or to help. How do you practice this phrase? You use this phrase to provide an explanation for the act of becoming the friend or assist. In order for Richard to enroll inside the specifically distinct membership, he need to befriend the leader.

beget

– To purpose or create. How do you follow this word? You use this word to describe some trouble this is the purpose of a few factor. Jealousy can frequently beget hostility, anger and sick will.

belated

– Late or behind schedule. How do you practice this phrase? You use this phrase to speak approximately some component that is overdue or behind schedule past the anticipated time. He grew to come to be in his belated English venture which modified into rejected.

belligerent

– Aggressively antagonistic and keen to fight. How do you have got a observe this word? You use this phrase to provide an reason behind someone who is ready to fight or argue and who's competitive. The greater beneath the have an effect on of alcohol he have end up, the greater belligerent he have end up with special bar customers.

benign

– Gentle or nice. How do you follow this word? You use this phrase to explain some thing that has a type and first-class. The medical doctor recommended him no longer to out of place any sleep, the tumor became small and extraordinarily benign.

bias

– To have prejudice in pick or in competition to 3 issue commonly in an unfair way. How do you exercise this phrase? You use this word to offer an reason for whilst a person is in prefer of a few element or in competition to some issue in an unfair and prejudice way. His bias did no longer without a doubt permit him to recognise what he end up talking approximately.

bigot

— Someone who's dedicated to his/her non-public beliefs, reviews or thoughts and is intolerant of others. How do you exercise this word? You use this word to describe someone who will not tolerate terrific opinions or thoughts and best devoted with their personal. It seems like bigotry plays a element in a few prepared faith.

bland

— Lacking one among a type or stimulating capabilities or flavor and is stupid. How do you comply with this phrase? You use this word to explain some factor stupid and stupid. The contents of his speech became bland in evaluation to the other audio device.

blatant

— Completely obvious or performed brazenly and unashamedly. How do you study this phrase? You use this phrase while you communicate about some thing apparent. The student failed to realise he had made a blatant errors on his test.

bluff

— An try to trick or deceive a person approximately one's abilities or intentions. How do you comply with this word? You use this word while a person or a few issue is making an attempt to misinform or trick especially about one's intentions. He recommended me he must pay me lower again double thru next week. I declined because I knew it became a bluff.

blunt

— Incredibly honest and certainly straightforward in speaking or tough in manners or speech. How do you observe this word? You use this phrase while talking approximately a person is easy, outspoken and abrupt of their speech. Matt end up typically very blunt in his conversations on the identical time as he modified into courting Sarah. She seemed to revel in his honesty.

bombard

— To attack a person constantly with phrases or speech. How do you have got a have a look at this phrase? You use this word to provide an cause of someone is attacking constantly with questions, thoughts, statements, phrases, and so forth. The president turn out to be bombarded with questions about his sex existence.

bond

— To be a part of or shape a dating based mostly on research, feelings or pastimes with someone else. How do you look at this word? You use this word while you're describing some component that brings people together. Our weekly softball video video games is an hobby that allowed our network to boom a stronger bond with each special.

boundless

— Having no bounds or limits. How do you comply with this phrase? You use this phrase even as describing some thing that is limitless or countless. What the thoughts can consider and create is boundless.

bravado

— A brave, assured display meant to affect however is pretended. How do you comply with this phrase? You use this phrase to provide an explanation for a faux show of self belief or bravery. His bravado modified into seemed down upon via using his buddies.

brief

— Short in time or in duration and concise. How do you exercise this phrase? You use this phrase to explain some detail that is brief in period and concise. He allowed his son Arnold to explain himself however to preserve it quick.

massive

— Covering a large scope; popular. How do you workout this phrase? You use this phrase at the same time as you are speaking typically with the purpose of protecting a big scope of subjects and regions. The student's requested the trainer for a extra effective solution after he gave a extensive one.

burden

— Something this is tough to bear and a terrific deliver of stress. How do you have a examine this word? You use this phrase at the same time as you're speakme approximately a few issue oppressive or hard to address. It became a super burden in the beginning for Max even as he come to be looking to lose fifty pounds.

Chapter 11: Candid

– Straightforward, honest and sincere. How do you observe this phrase? When you are attempting to describe a few issue or a person as frank and real. His candid approach to education era inspired college college college students to have a study greater.

capable

– Having the electricity or functionality to perform a little factor. How do you observe this word? You use this word to explain a person or some component that has the capability to acquire or perform a bit aspect. After schooling for 3 grueling months, he turn out to be greater capable of finishing the as soon as a one year marathon.

cater

– To provide or supply meals, offerings or amusement. How do you study this phrase? You use this word to present an explanation for a few factor or someone who attends to the dreams or desires of. Before the wedding, Curt had to undergo in mind to pay greater for catering.

surrender

— To prevent or placed an give up to. How do you exercise this phrase? You use this phrase to intend stop or positioned an forestall to. In order for him to shed kilos, he needed to stop consuming fast food three times regular with week.

celibacy

— Abstaining from sexual own family individuals. How do you check this word? You use this word to explain someone who chooses not to have intercourse. Jane determined to exercise celibacy due to the truth she felt it have become the right component to do.

cellulite

— A lumpy, fatty deposit within the thighs and on the buttocks. How do you check this phrase? You use this phrase to describe or speaking about the fatty areas at the human body. Jessica modified into very touchy approximately her weight and he or she have grow to be indignant at the same time as everybody noted her cellulite.

chastise

– To punish or criticize drastically. How do you observe this word? When you speak about inflicting punishment or giving or receiving complaint. His mother chastised him each time he stayed out too overdue.

cherish

– To protect or care for in a loving way. How do you practice this phrase? You use this phrase while you need to provide an reason for someone who holds some issue or someone high-priced. Philip genuinely loved the reminiscences he had along along together with his uncle throughout special fishing trips.

cite

– To refer a passage, ebook or creator as proof or in help of a controversy or announcement. How do you follow this phrase? You use this word to provide an explanation for wherein you bought a particular quote or passage. Can you inform me in which you referred to that passage from?

coherent

– Capable of logical and regular speech, concept, and so forth; capable to talk really and logically. How do you've got a study this phrase? You use this phrase while speaking about a few factor that sounds rational and logical. Trevor made a very coherent case protecting the sufferer.

coincide

– To stand up at the equal time or to be in settlement. How do you look at this phrase? You use this while you communicate about some aspect that happens on the same time. I had a scientific scientific doctors appointment that coincided with my daughters piano recital. I had to re-time table.

commend

– To precise approval of or to praise as surely worth or ideal

How do you comply with this word? You use this word at the same time as you describing the expression or motion of expressing approval or reward. His bodily teacher recommended him on his 10 pound weight lose.

complacent

– Extremely self-happy and pleased, specially with oneself

How do you take a look at this word? You use this word whilst describing someone who is conceited, thrilled with themselves or self-happy. Greg turn out to be complacent after making his selection to purchase his home.

complaint

– an expression of pain, pain or discontent. How do you study this phrase? You use this word at the identical time as you are speaking approximately some thing that reasons pain, grief or dissatisfaction. After receiving his meal, he had some court docket instances about it.

complement

– A man or woman or component that completes a few aspect, fills up or makes best. How do you have a look at this word? You use this phrase at the same time as you are describing some element that completes some issue or makes some aspect whole. Purchasing purple wine with the meal truely complements the whole revel in.

complete

— Including and protecting all or nearly all factors or elements of a few aspect. How do you check this phrase? You use this word on the equal time as speakme approximately a few factor that includes a huge scope or a vast type of elements about a few aspect. He wrote the most entire ebook on biology I've ever check.

concede

— To admit some thing is real or valid after denying it or resisting it or to sincerely admit to be actual or valid. How do you follow this word? You use this phrase even as you admit a few thing as being actual or legitimate. It can also mean to give up. After an prolonged grueling hour of arguing, he ultimately conceded with me.

idea

— Something this is common within the thoughts collectively with thoughts, mind or plans. How do you check this phrase? You use this word whilst speaking approximately an idea or idea this is created and usual within the mind. She seemed to have weird conceptions about the manner to make her bakery industrial corporation flourish yet again.

concise

— Giving or expressing pretty some facts simply in few terms; short but complete. How do you follow this phrase? You use this word whilst describing a person who expresses hundreds however the utilization of few phrases. Cindy gave a concise rationalization of what The Great Gatsby was approximately to the class.

conditioned

— To trade or make a few component appropriate for a wonderful cause. How do you comply with this word? You use this word to provide an cause of a few trouble that makes some issue great or suitable for a fantastic cause or cause. Tim idea he had been conditioned to shop for soda because of the severa commercials he noticed selling it.

condone

— To permit, approve or forgive a few factor especially if a few element is wrong or unlawful to keep. How do you have a study this word? You use this phrase to talk approximately a few issue you do or do no longer take delivery of and allow despite the fact that it's incorrect. As a vegan, he's in competition to the slaughter of animals and does not condone the killing and ingesting of them.

confide

— To inform a person a thriller or private rely and troubles; to have whole remember in. How do you observe this word? You use this phrase even as speaking approximately sharing secrets and techniques and private topics or having entire agree with in. Chris in the end confided in his therapist after months of seeing him.

conform

– To comply with and follow policies, requirements and prison recommendations. How do you practice this phrase? You use this word at the same time as you are describing a person who follows and abides through recommendations, standards or prison hints. Peter said he did not in reality comply with Sally's spiritual beliefs.

conniving

– Plotting to do a little element wrongful or unlawful in mystery. How do you follow this phrase? When you're describing a person who is making plans to do a little thing immoral or dangerous. The evil villain became constantly conniving the down fall of the hero.

consent

– To agree, permit or approve of a few element. How do you observe this word? You use this phrase whilst you're talking about some component that you agree or do not agree to. The man who was pulled over through the police did no longer consent to any searches.

effect

– A end that follows some element logically or simply from a motion or state of affairs. How do you exercising this phrase? You use this phrase even as you communicate approximately the stop end result of an movement or the belief that certainly follows a few difficulty. By disobeying her parents, she had to face the consequences

constitute

– To make up, compose or form. How do you've got a study this phrase? You use this word at the same time as you need to talk about subjects that form or make up some thing. Believing in a few aspect without a proof would not constitute a valid, low-priced argument.

constraint

– A limitation or limit. How do you take a look at this word? You use this word when you are speaking about a restriction or a stress avoided to restriction and dictate the movement or mind of. My low self perception and self-doubt has been a intense constraint with regards to getting peace and happiness in my life.

construe

– To offer or give an explanation for the meaning or purpose of; to interpret a phrase or motion in a certain way. How do you practice this phrase? You use this word to speak about the reason of the which means or aim of a few difficulty. In my English magnificence, the teacher recited Shakespeare sonnets. A majority of the scholars had trouble construing what they supposed.

ponder

– To reflect onconsideration on or have a examine, thoughtfully and deeply. How do you follow this word? You use this word to intend carefully considering some thing or thinking about very well and deeply. Strong ideals became all preserve, have to no longer be disregarded but want to be contemplated and analyzed.

contradict

– To assert the possibility of some element or be inconsistent with. How do you practice this phrase? You use this phrase while spotting thoughts, thoughts or statements which might be contrary with every special. He weakened his fighters argument through bringing up the numerous contradictions that had been in it.

opposite

– Opposed or contrary in route or characteristic. How do you examine this phrase? You use this phrase at the same time as you're talking approximately a few issue is opposite of something. Contrary to what most people receive as right with, writing might now not must be very difficult to do.

convoluted

— Complicated or tough to comprehend. How do you workout this phrase? You use this word whilst talking approximately something this is hard to apprehend or a few thing this is very complicated. His book featured many convoluted standards on genetics.

covert

— Concealed or thriller and no openly displayed, practiced or engaged in. How do you practice this phrase? When speakme approximately a few aspect that isn't openly practiced or engaged in. He hypnotized the target market the usage of unlawful covert methods.

coy

— Pretending to be shy or modest with the purpose of being flirtatious. How do you look at this word? You use this phrase to describe a person who is shy or modest. Rachel has a dishonest to be coy mainly round guys.

crux

— A essential, important or applicable detail or function; a tough or hard problem. How do you examine this phrase? You use this phrase at the same time as describing or speakme approximately the main, precious difficulty of some thing. He told me that phase A have emerge as the crux of the whole document.

credible

— Capable of being believed. How do you study this phrase? You use this phrase to explain some thing this is reliable, plausible and honest. Some humans think Wikipedia is not a good supply of statistics.

culinary

— Relating to a kitchen or cooking. How do you exercising this phrase? You use this phrase even as you're regarding some issue that has to do with cooking or a few detail used inside the kitchen. My friend cautioned me that the cooking beauty he had with Gordon Ramsay modified into a remarkable culinary revel in.

wrongdoer

— Someone who is responsible for a crime, fault or offense; a supply or reason of a trouble. How do you follow this phrase? When you're speakme approximately a person who's liable for a particular offense or fault. The 5 cookies have been missing. She knew Billy turned into the culprit.

bulky

— Difficult or tough to cope with. How do you observe this word? You use this word at the same time as speaking about some factor that is difficult to cope with. She concept to herself having six children may be cumbersome at instances.

curtail

— To lessen brief, reduce or lessen; to reduce a detail off. How do you practice this word? You use this phrase even as you're speaking about some factor that grow to be, is or going to be lessen short reduced or lessened. Due to time constraint's, Curtis needed to curtail his presentation on nuclear waste.

cynical

— Bitterly distrustful of the motives of others or dubious as to whether or not or no longer or no longer some issue will arise; sarcastic or mocking. How do you exercise this phrase? You use this phrase at the same time as you are speakme about a person who is very distrustful and contemptuous of the reasons of others. You additionally may be talking about some thing who is awful or a pessimist. Pablo has a cynical view of the president's plans to better the u . S ..

dabble

— To take part in a few thing casually without critical purpose. How do you have a look at this phrase? You use this word at the equal time as you're talking approximately doing some aspect casually in an amateurish way. My father dabbled within the stock market for a few months but placed it stressful.

dainty

— Something that is proper to consume or delicately lovely. How do you practice this phrase? You use this phrase whilst describing some component this is scrumptious, attractive to the taste buds or a few aspect that is delicately fascinating and delightful. Michelle cherished choosing up dainty plants in her mothers garden.

debacle

– An abrupt, disastrous collapse, failure, or defeat. How do you study this word? You use it even as speaking approximately a incident that ended with disaster, failure or defeat. Tony confronted a debacle after he emerge as stuck stealing from his interest.

debunk

– To expose the falseness or exaggerated claims of. How do you test this phrase? You use this phrase whilst you are speakme approximately the act of revealing some thing as fake or incorrect. James Randi seems at the way to debunk anyone who makes crazy, supernatural claims.

decipher

– Trying to have a study, interpret or decode. How do you examine this phrase? You use this phrase when you are attempting to discover the because of this of a few difficulty specifically some thing difficult. His handwriting modified into so illegible, it took me an hour to decipher it.

decrepit

— Weakened or wiped out through the use of vintage age, lengthy use or forget about. How do you exercising this word? You use this word whilst you want to provide an explanation for some element worn out or susceptible because of vintage age. Mike had a certainly vintage boombox that emerge as decrepit and seldom worked anymore.

deduction

— A end drawn from reasoning or the act of subtracting a few component. How do you have a look at this word? You use this word to call a give up you get from reasoning. Sally said the soup wanted extra tomato sauce. That have become he deduction.

deem

— To count on, determine or have an opinion on. How do you examine this word? You use this phrase at the same time as you are attempting to mention select or assume. He deemed it merciless to euthanize unwanted pets.

definitive

— Authoritative, maximum dependable and complete. How do you have a look at this word? When describing some problem that is reliable and gives a very remaining solution for. He wrote the definitive manual at the manner to supply be a better public speaker.

deliberate

— Carefully considered; intentional. How do you take a look at this phrase? You use this word at the same time as you are speakme about a few problem this is intentional or performed with careful consideration. Jane intentionally attempted to butt in a non-public communication I grow to be having.

delineate

— To depict, portray or describe in phrases or gestures particularly with detail. How do you workout this phrase? You use this word whilst you're speakme about portraying or representing some component. Jessica's mother had to delineate the strict rules yet again.

delude

— To misinform or misinform the thoughts or judgment of; to impose a misleading perception upon someone. How do you observe this word? You use this phrase while you're talking about a person being tricked or deceive. She have emerge as very deluded approximately numerous religious ideals.

demeanor

– The manner a person behaves. How do you observe this phrase? You use this word when you want to speak about the way a person conducts themselves. His demeanor changed into usually calm and cushty but on the internal it was one-of-a-kind.

demographic

– A specific section or company of the population. How do you study this phrase? You use this word to label a positive segment/s of the population. Justin Timberlake caters to a specific demographic than Miles Davis does.

demonstrable

– Capable of being established or proved. How do you examine this phrase? You use this phrase while you are speakme about a few aspect that is apparent and obvious or capable of be established and proved. The criminal suggestions of gravity and physics may be demonstrable.

demoralize

— To undermine or weaken the self guarantee or morale of. How do you comply with this word? You use this word whilst speakme approximately a few detail that lowers or weakens the self perception of. Jake concept it have grow to be demoralize for his mother to bitch about how he lives.

denial

— A refusal to comply with or fulfill a request. How do you comply with this phrase? You use this phrase whilst a person refuses to satisfy a declare, request or preference or the refusal of the individual making it. He have become in denial approximately shaving his head because of his receding hairline.

depict

— To display or constitute in a image, drawing, illustration or to symbolize by means of way of terms. How do you have a look at this phrase? You use this word to mean constitute. Most of the depictions of Jesus Christ display him having extended hair.

dissipate

– To dissipate or to decrease the deliver of. How do you practice this phrase? You use this word even as some factor diminishes or makes use of up some thing till its empty. My video game man or woman depleted his health and died.

derive

– To gain or get maintain of from a source. How do you look at this phrase? You use this word whilst speakme about some component that is won or acquired from a specific deliver or starting. His favorite costs to live thru had been derived from the Bible.

however

– In spite of. How do you examine this phrase? You use this phrase at the same time as you need to say no matter. He favored to workout yoga regardless of getting a damaged arm.